Understanding Multi-Level
and Their Role in a Successful Company

by Mark Rawlins
Founder and President, InfoTrax Systems, Inc.

InfoTrax Systems, Inc.
1815 South State Street, Suite 4500
Orem, UT 84097
Phone (801) 802-8729
Fax (801) 802-7408
www.infotraxsystems.com

© November 4, 2008, Mark Rawlins

Note: This book is intended to offer general information on the subject matter covered. Although the multi-level commissions issues are believed to be accurate, some material may be affected by changes in law.

The author assumes no responsibility for errors or omissions. The author specifically disclaims any liability resulting from the use or application of the information contained in this book. If legal or other expert advice is needed or appropriate, the reader is strongly encouraged to obtain the services of a professional expert.

© Mark Rawlins
All Rights Reserved. No part of this book may be reproduced or transmitted in any form or by any means, electronic or mechanical, including photocopying, recording, or by any information storage and retrieval system, without permission in writing from the author.

ISBN 978-0-9717536-1-7
InfoTrax Systems, Inc.
1815 South State Street, Suite 4500
Orem, UT 84097
Phone (801) 802-8729
Fax (801) 802-7408
www.infotraxsystems.com

Revised Edition: November 2008

Dedication

To Kerri, the best wife a man could have, who showed infinite patience and held our family together during my "workaholic, absentee husband and father" decade while I was off learning the ins and outs of network marketing software. She has certainly earned her share of whatever success comes to us.

To my parents, Julia and Lindsay Rawlins, whose commitment to making sure their children had a better life than they did and provided me the education, opportunity, and support to start my own business. To my children, Kenny, Christopher, Anthony, Whitney, and Jeffrey, who swear they won't hold my absentee years against me (although they do always mention a trust fund in the same sentence).

Acknowledgements

A number of people have offered invaluable assistance to me in the creation of this book. I owe thanks to the people of InfoTrax Systems: For help with content, Glen Rawlins and Nancy Tobler; the two best commission plan programmers in the world, Devry Anderson and Ray Rawlins; Leroy Ball for production work on the book under harrowing conditions; and Juli Wilkins for keeping us all on track.

Special thanks also to Robyn Openshaw-Pay of OP Publishing for showing me what the project could be, and Barbara R. Hume of TechVoice, Inc. who spent many hours helping me, organizing my thoughts, and digging in for the details for the writing and organization.

Table of Contents

Preface: How can this book help me? ix

Section One: What You Need to Know First

Chapter One: Network marketing and methods of distribution . . 3
    Traditional sales, direct sales, and network marketing 3
    The cornerstones: successful network marketing company..... 7
    How network marketing has changed....................... 20

Chapter Two: What do you need to know about distributors? . 27
    The five types of distributors 28
    Sales commissions 33
    Sales management commissions........................... 34
    The effect of commission plans on distributor behavior 35
    Why people join network marketing companies.............. 37
    Rules of network marketing commission plans............... 39

Chapter Three: Where do you begin? 47
    Five steps to a commission plan design 48

Section Two: The Building Blocks

Chapter Four: Types of commissions / Commission plans 61
    Overview 61
    Level commissions 62
    Differential commissions 75
    Single-level commissions................................... 82
    Pool commissions.. 85
    Conclusion.. 88

Chapter Five: Rules that govern commission plans 93
    The four kinds of rules 93
    Rank advancement rules 95
    Reversion.. 101
    Monthly qualification rules................................ 104
    Other rules to consider.................................... 106

Summary 107

Chapter Six: How does structure affect commission plans? ... 111
    Reasons for structure requirements 112
    Types of structure requirements........................... 114
    Summary 122

Chapter Seven: Other miscellaneous commissions 125
    Overview 125
    Matching Commissions 125
    Automobile Shared Pool Commissions 126
    Fast-start commissions 129
    Incentive Programs 130
    Summary 131

Chapter Eight: Operational issues & network marketing 135
    Overview 135
    Pricing.. 135
    Reduced commission value products 137
    International Commissions................................ 138
    Open Enrollment vs. Barriers-to-Signup 141
    Open enrollment 141
    Barriers to signup....................................... 144

Section Three: Putting Everything Together

Chapter Nine: The most common commission plans........... 151
    Overview 151
    Review... 153
    Party plans.. 154
    Traditional network marketing............................ 155
    Stairstep 156
    Unigen... 160
    Unilevel... 164
    Hybrid Unilevel 168
    Matrix 172
    Binary 175

Conclusion 180

Chapter Ten: What commission plans are designed for 185
Overview 185
Creating a commission plan earnings emphasis 185
Sales management commissions. 197

Chapter Eleven: What is the future of commission plans?..... 205
Conclusion 210
A Unique Perspective—Mark's Own 224
InfoTrax Systems. 229
Conclusion 232

Section Four: Appendices

Appendix A: Glossary. 213

Appendix B: Bio of Mark Rawlins 223

Appendix C: InfoTrax and Distributor Confidence 227

Appendix D: Commission plan Payout: Exercises 235
Paying Commissions with a Unilevel Commission plan 236
Unilevel with No Compression. 238
Unilevel with Standard Compression, Examples 3 and 4..... 242
Unilevel Standard Compression, Examples 5 and 6 245
Unilevel with Dynamic Compression, Examples 7 and 8 249
Stairstep Differential 254

Appendix E: The Internet and Network Marketing 263

Index 267

Understanding Multi-Level Commissions

How can this book help me?

Why I wrote the book

In 1981, as a junior programmer, I programmed my first network marketing commission plan. What a beauty! Unilevel in structure, it paid five percent down six levels on a $25.00 per month service (compression had not yet been invented). I attended company meetings and got caught up in the excitement. I just knew that it was only a matter of time until someone made $20,000 or even $30,000 a month!

Each month, I ran the checks and watched the top ones grow. And grow they did—until they stalled at about $3,000 a month. Shortly thereafter, the company stalled.

The lesson I learned from this experience was that in a simple unilevel plan, people stack; therefore, sales volume moves out of a distributor's pay level very quickly. The potential payout that people think they will earn is never even remotely achieved.

This was the first of dozens of such lessons I learned in working with more than 200 companies in the last twenty years.

In 1985, I was working with a company that wanted to decrease its number of qualified leaders in order to increase the value of the individual shares of its leadership commission pool. The decision was made to double the amount of sales volume required to become a leader and double the monthly qualifying volume. The following month, the number of qualified leaders did not decrease—in fact, it increased by fifty percent! Although the company failed in its goal of increasing the leadership pool because the value of the individual shares of the leadership pool diminished by ten percent, within two years the company's sales had increased five-fold! Because sales went up, all the other commissions went up as well.

Another fascinating lesson learned – the law of unintended consequences. When people believe that there's a lot of money to be made, they dive in and work very hard. So, by extension, sometimes qualifying volume can, in fact, be too low.

Because of my unique position of working with marketers and then seeing the effect that changes to the commission plans they make, not just for one company but for a couple of hundred—I've gained a perspective shared by only a handful of people. For years, as president of InfoTrax Systems (a provider of software to the network marketing industry, but that's another story; see www.infotraxsys.com), I have consulted with companies, sharing the knowledge gained as a result of these and many other experiences. Unlike someone who designs commission plans from scratch and therefore tends to work with a few types of plans, the majority of my consulting is taking a plan that has already been designed and making it work. You could compare this to what engineers do once an architect has designed a building; they take over and figure out how to make things like heating, elevators, and electrical systems work. As a result, I have worked with every type of plan in existence. I'm writing this book to give anyone who wants to understand how commissions work a good foundation on the basics of commission plans. This book doesn't contain everything you need to know, but it's a starting point.

In my consulting career, I've always made a practice of trying to give advice that's grounded in experience. This advice is based on theories that have been tested at enough companies to prove them out. I don't think that you have done well by a company if you bet their future on an idea that hasn't been proven out by the marketplace. In this book, you'll see sidebars in which I get "On the Soapbox." These sidebars deal with my ideas and concepts that haven't necessarily been proven by the marketplace. In the body of the book, I try to stick to the tried-and-true facts that I've seen through twenty years of providing software and consulting.

Over the past ten years, it has become increasingly clear to me that it's just as important for network marketing distributors to understand these concepts. Why? Because distributors invest their all into building a downline. In the first example, I showed you that the distributors worked night and day for almost three years, thinking there was an opportunity to earn an income that simply was not there! And I, however unknowingly, was part of that deception. I'm writing this book because I know that if distributors understand these concepts, they can make better choices about the companies in which to invest their lives.

Preface

After I spent nearly ten years thinking about writing this book, the catalyst for getting started on the project was being asked to help create the curriculum for a course on direct sales/network marketing for the School of Business at Utah Valley State College (www.uvsc.edu). Thanks to this endeavor, I finally gathered together all of my miscellaneous memos, my videotaped talks, and the notes from my seminars. With these materials as a basis, I have written the book.

Network marketing commission plans are difficult to set up. More than that—they're difficult to understand in the first place. Plenty of individuals who've been involved in the network marketing industry for years are still struggling to understand their company's commission plan. As with anything else, greater knowledge leads to better decisions about your commission plan.

Why are commission plans so important? Because if a company sets them up thoughtlessly, without considering all the ramifications that affect payout and distributor behavior, it can find itself with a wildly successful company whose very success puts it right out of business! Such a disaster has happened more than once in this industry. Or the company could end up with what I call a "hollow" plan—lots of distributors, but few sales.

In this book, I'll show what does and doesn't work in terms of commission plans. I'll show you what I've learned through years of hard experience. Changes come and go in the industry, but the underlying needs of plans remain constant and necessary to success.

Throughout this book, I'll discuss the effects that various commission plan elements have on distributor behavior. A poorly conceived commission plan can result in the kind of widespread distributor defection that stops a network marketing company dead in its tracks. The truth is that once a company figures out how to recruit, the biggest challenge in this industry is finding ways of maintaining distributor loyalty.

In this book, then, we'll take a look at commission plans and why they are the way they are. We'll examine the various components of a network marketing commission plan—its *commissions*, its *rules*, and its *structures*—and we'll discover how they all work together. By the time it's all over, you should have a clear understanding of how different aspects of various commission plans can affect a company's performance.

After all, *your* company is the one you really want to succeed.

And now, here it is—*the* book on understanding multi-level commissions and their role in a successful company.

Section One: What you need to know first

In this first section, I discuss the background of network marketing. In Chapter One, we talk about the history of the industry and what has changed through the years. In Chapter Two, we take a look at distributors, why they join companies, and why they do what they do. The final chapter of this section, Chapter Three, is a little different from the rest of the book in that it discusses *how* to design a commission plan. This information may be interesting to you if you're trying to decide what company to join, but it won't be the most crucial information you get from this book.

So now that you know what you're getting into, let's get on with Section One.

Chapter One

Key Topics

Traditional sales, direct sales, and network marketing 3
The cornerstones of a successful company 7
   I. Products 8
      Intellectual distribution of product 10
      What products and services work? 12
      What products and services don't work? 15
   II. Services 16
   III. Communications... 16
   IV. Distributor commissions. 19
How network marketing has changed........................ 20
   Computers. 20
   Product Delivery. 20
   Communications... 21
   Videos and audiotapes..................................... 21
   Internet. 21

Understanding Multi-Level Commissions

How is network marketing different from other methods of distribution?

Traditional sales, direct sales, and network marketing

Let's begin by clearing up a couple of misconceptions that have dogged the network marketing industry for years:

1. A network marketing company has almost nothing in common with a traditional sales organization – True.
2. A network marketing company has almost everything in common with a traditional sales organization – Also true.

Once you understand this apparent contradiction, you'll be well on your way to understanding network marketing commission plans. Everything that applies in a traditional sales organization also applies in network marketing. It just applies in a very different manner. Companies still have to motivate people. They still have to manage people. They still have to pay people to sell product. They just go about it in very different ways than in a traditional sales environment.

Every successful commission plan has two basic elements to manage:

- Pay those who sell the product a fair commission so they will wish to continue selling for the company.
- Pay those who manage the sales process so they will wish to continue motivating and supporting the sales force.

The process of taking a product to market through a traditional sales force relies on salespeople, who explain and sell the product while addressing their consumers' needs; sales managers, who work with and train salespeople; and motivators, the people who generate and maintain enthusiasm.

In this sense, network marketing and a traditional sales force are similar. How each goes about accomplishing the product-to-market process, however, marks their dissimilarity. In a traditional sales organization, the work is done by employees who are hired, fired, promoted, or demoted. The marketing department does its job, and the salespeople do their jobs.

In network marketing, a product is distributed by a volunteer army of distributors who choose which markets to enter or leave, whether to spend their time selling product or building their organizations, and whether to work part-time or full-time.

Some of the subjects I discuss in this book may surprise you. Why, for example, should I discuss product in a book devoted to commission plans? Because a clear understanding of commission plans requires an understanding of the relationship between the four cornerstones of a network marketing company:

1. The product or service the company sells
2. The services the company provides to its distributors and consumers
3. The company's communications strategy
4. The company's commission plan

Although my focus is commission plans, an understanding of how commissions affect the other three cornerstones is essential to grasping the complex and multi-faceted nature of why and how a commission plan works. Therefore, in order to instill a sense of how commission plans operate within all areas of a network marketing business, I will discuss how commission plans support or hinder each of the other cornerstones.

Before we begin, I want to clarify a couple of terms I'll be using throughout this book. It's important for you to have a clear understanding of the way I use the terms "direct sales company" and "network marketing company," often called an "MLM" or "multi-level marketing" company. Another term I will use often throughout the book is party plan.

According to the Direct Selling Association, "In direct selling, products or services are marketed to consumers by independent salespeople person-to-person. Depending on the company, the salespeople may be called distributors, representatives, consultants or various other titles. Products are sold primarily through in-home product demonstrations, parties, and one-on-one selling." (DSA web site: www.dsa.org.) These companies don't sell by means of traditional storefronts or direct mailings or telemarketing or mass media advertising. Rather, they sell by means of independent representatives, often called distributors. I use the term "distributor" throughout, but remember that I refer to these independent representatives, not to a jobber such as a book distributor. Direct sales distributors are usually required to use the term "independent representative" on their business cards to make their status clear.

Network marketing companies are a *type* of direct sales company. These companies, in addition to paying their distributors to sell products, also encourage the distributors to recruit downline distributors by paying commissions on the sales of their downline distributors.

Party plan companies are another type of direct sales company. These companies focus on in-home product demonstrations and employ several other business practices that distinguish them from traditional network marketing companies. The reason I discuss these companies is that more and more of them are paying multi-level commissions.

Figure 1

To keep all of this straight, the two types of companies that pay multi-level commissions are *traditional network marketing companies* and *party plan companies*. Many people call either of one of these a "multi-level" company, which is technically correct. The only reason I refer to them exclusively by the terms "network marketing" or "party plan" companies as well as multi-level commission plans is to increase clarity.

So what's the difference between a network marketing company and a traditional business that employs salespeople to sell directly to consumers? A traditional retail organization is exclusively *sales-oriented*; if you sell for such a company, you make your money exclusively from sales and sales commissions. Only the sale matters.

Another consideration is that in traditional businesses such as automobile dealerships and insurance companies, the salespeople are *employees*. They may be on commission, but they're hired, promoted, and fired just as they would be in any other job.

A network marketing company bases a distributor's earnings on both personal sales and sales generated by the distributor's organization—the people they recruit. Unlike the single income stream of traditional sales companies, network marketers have a dual income stream: income from personal volume sales commissions *and* commissions on group volume sales from their downline.

Unlike the traditional business, an independent distributor with a network marketing company is not a hired employee. The distributor is in charge of his or her own career choices—whether to make a few hundred dollars extra each month, a few thousand, or tens of thousands by building a large organization. He or she can also choose to work part-time, and as long as the company requirements are met, the distributor can remain with the company.

So you can see that a network marketing company's commission plan is likely to be more complex than that of a retail establishment or, for that matter, a traditional direct sales company.

You will find additional terminology specific to the network marketing industry in the glossary of terms in Appendix A.

The cornerstones of a successful network marketing company

A network marketing company needs balance. The four cornerstones on which a company builds its business are:

1. *products*
2. *services*
3. *communications*
4. *commissions*

These cornerstones support and uphold virtually every aspect of a company. Once the company has established these cornerstones, they've defined the company's architecture and foundation—the basis for the company's culture. From this point forward, *almost every decision and policy* they initiate will be a direct result of the company's cornerstones.

The cornerstones of a network marketing company must correspond to and reinforce one another. No company will succeed without a good product; none can succeed without taking into account the need to take care of its distributors (the "services" part of the equation). If a company can't communicate what it's trying to accomplish, what's the point? And without a good commission plan, the company is in deep trouble from the very beginning.

Let's look at the four cornerstones of network marketing.

I. Products

What role does the product play? I want to discuss the fact that certain kinds of products are suitable for network marketing and why. The product should be something that requires motivation, education, training, or support to use. It often represents a great leap forward in some way. In other words, the consumer needs some form of training.

A company should plan to market a product its people believe in and feel proud of. When someone says to me, "The product a company sells doesn't matter," I see that person as looking for a scam. Because, of course, *product does matter*. Legitimate company founders want to contribute to the welfare of the society they live in by selling products that have real value.

The needs of consumers change. A network marketing company may build its success on a product or product line because it doesn't have general market acceptance. Innovative products have often used the network marketing venue to enter the market. Distributors make people aware of the value of these products and educate them in correct usage. The products and the distribution method serve each other.

In addition to having products that use the strengths of network marketing, it's important to understand that people become distributors because they subscribe to a company's mission. "What if a company doesn't have a mission?" you may ask. But the fact is, *it does*. Even if the company owners don't know what it is, the product line the company sells, and the way the company sells it, creates a mission in the distributors' minds.

So why is it important for a company to know what its mission is? Because someday the company management is going to want to expand the product line. Or the product they've been selling may be mainstreamed and no longer appropriate for network marketing, and the company must change the product line altogether. When the company does this, *if the new product fits within the mission* and *if the commission plan they designed supports this new product line*, the company will be fine. But if it's a complete departure, acceptance can be difficult. Some companies believe their distributor network would distribute any product they decided to sell. This approach doesn't work. If a company is planning to broaden its product line, it needs to be sure its mission allows for it.

As a company looks at its products, it must consider numerous issues, such as:

1. Price points
2. Amount available for commissions
3. Percentage of the population that might buy the product
4. Socio-economic profile of their consumers
5. Time, effort, and knowledge required to sell this product to a consumer (cost of consumer acquisition)
6. What other related products the company might sell to that consumer
7. Whether the product is consumable
8. Whether the product requires high motivation/support, high education/training, or both

Remember—any success a company has that is not built on product value and the loyalty of its distributors to its products is fleeting at best. I often hear from employees of successful companies, "We're not like other companies. Our distributors are loyal to our product." Hearing this comment always makes me smile, because virtually every company that has experienced long-term success is built on product loyalty. So what kinds of products inspire loyalty and work best in the network marketing industry? Read on.

> *In the end, a company only survives if it has great products. The reality is that for every distributor you pay $50,000 a month, there are at least a thousand consumers you pay nothing. The only reason those thousand will stay is for the product. – Winston Lambert, Top Unicity Sales Leader*

Intellectual distribution of product

The amount of product sold via direct sales has exploded during the past twenty years. Paul Zane Pilzer's book, *The Next Trillion*, provides an excellent overview of the economic realities that have caused this incredible growth. (You can order *The Next Trillion* at www.thenexttrillion.com or find an expanded version in bookstores under the title *The Wellness Revolution: How to Make a Fortune in the Next Trillion Dollar Industry*).

In the book, Pilzer explains that the basic principle in the sales process consists of two parts: *intellectual distribution* and *physical distribution*.

The process of physical distribution is simply getting the product into the hands of the consumer. On the other hand, intellectual distribution requires teaching potential consumers what the product does and how it can help them. In other words, intellectual distribution is *education*.

Because intellectual distribution represents the best opportunity for network marketing companies to succeed, I have created what I call The METS Formula (Motivate, Educate, Train, Support):

Motivation. For some products, such as diet or health products, distributors may need to spend time motivating consumers to start using them and to stay with them.

Education. Why is your product better than competing products? Why should consumers spend their money on your product rather than on one of the many others out there? Or why do your consumers need those products at all? Education about product is essential to a company's success.

Training. Some products require *training* for the consumer to use them effectively.

Support. Finally, some products require ongoing *support* from the distributor for the consumer to know how to use it.

In my experience, the products or services that are best suited to network marketing require one or more aspects of the METS formula. So why has network marketing had such explosive growth in the last thirty years?

Throughout history, almost everyone selling products educated consumers about the products they sold. Such is no longer the case. Beginning in the 1960s, Sam Walton discovered that physical distribution is a good deal easier and much cheaper than intellectual distribution. He therefore chose to ignore intellectual distribution and concentrate on lowering the cost of physical distribution. As a result, he stopped selling products that required intellectual distribution, creating Wal-Mart, one of the largest corporations in the world. This approach gave rise to the "discount superstore," a concept that *decreased* the cost of everyday items, but *also decreased the outlets for innovative new products that required intellectual distribution*.

What about products that require intellectual distribution? Some products are simply not intuitive, are too new for people to be comfortable using on their own, or require consumer assistance. Given the ever-growing number of new products that require motivation, education, training, and support, it was essential to carve out new channels of distribution or expand old ones.

Network marketing, of course, is one of these channels. Other popular channels include:

- Infomercials (kitchen devices, fitness products)
- Category busters (megastores such as PetSmart or HomeBase)
- Paid salespeople at retail establishments (automobile dealerships, cell phones, home computers)
- Independent franchises (insurance, financial planning)

There are other advantages to combining intellectual distribution with physical distribution. Companies that teach consumers how to use their products and services are more likely to build a cadre of committed consumers. (For a more in-depth explanation of this concept, see Chapter Five of Paul Zane Pilzer's *The Next Trillion*.)

What products and services work for network marketing?

The question is, what makes a product or service that requires intellectual distribution appropriate for network marketing? Look again at the METS Formula. Traditionally, network marketing seems to work best for products that require some, but not extensive, education and training, but that do require a lot of motivation and/or support.

For example, my wife enjoys the home decorating parties and scrapbooking parties hosted by distributors of some of today's successful network marketing companies. Her friends are there, she has a good time socially, she gets new ideas, and she has her own choices validated. For the company, success comes when she enjoys redecorating the living room so much that she then wants to do five more rooms in the house.

My wife's decorating parties rely on the elements of motivation and support. Obviously, the distributor requires some education in order to hold a successful party, but such education and training typically requires only a few hours a month. (It's important that this training not require too much time, since most distributors are part-time.) Often, the company assumes the task of educating and training consumers so that the distributors can concentrate on motivation and support.

Over the past twenty years, network marketing companies have followed this basic procedure. And recently, thanks to new technologies such as web-based meetings and conference calls, it has become easier to do. And, although only a few companies are taking advantage of the opportunity so far, the Internet is enabling great leaps in this area. (See Appendix E for a more in-depth discussion of ways to use the Internet to provide education and training quickly and easily.) As network marketing companies take over more and more of the education and training of consumers, the spectrum of products that these companies sell will broaden.

Other products for which motivation and support are vital are beauty products, diet products, and health products. These types of products need accompanying motivation and support because so many choices are available that consumers may have difficulty in choosing. We must assume that potential consumers have tried many times, without success, to change their lives. In order to interest them in a product, the distributor must be able to present someone they can relate to who has been successfully changed by the product. Another factor is that charlatans have sold so many worthless products in these arenas that potential consumers are wary of trying yet another unless it has the endorsement of someone they trust.

Finally, a product is suitable for network marketing if it's a new product or falls into a new category that people are not yet familiar with. Often, they don't even know why they need it! In this case, often a recommendation from a friend will help them make the decision.

Obviously, there's no reason to build a network marketing company to distribute, for example, a run-of-the-mill toothbrush. Anyone can walk into a drugstore or grocery store and purchase one, not to mention the one the dentist gives you for free when you get your teeth cleaned! Your mother or your dentist has already taught you how to use a toothbrush. You don't need a distributor to bring one over to you and demonstrate the fine points of toothbrush wielding, or warn you against improper toothbrush usage. As in this example, a product about which the consumer already has all the information he or she needs is not suitable for network marketing. A product that the consumer can pick up on any casual trip to the grocery store or to the mall is not suitable. You need to sell a product with *differentiation*—something that makes it stand out from other products.

The problem, of course, is that if a product achieves general market acceptance, sooner or later, it will show up on the shelves of discount superstores. At that point, a company must either find new ways to *differentiate its product* or *develop a new product* for distribution. Over the years, we've witnessed this kind of product-shifting from network marketing to retail sales outlets with protein drinks, aloe vera, anti-oxidants, herbal supplements, fiber supplements, and many other products.

The computer industry has witnessed its share of product shifting, too. In the early 1980s, when the notion of a home computer was novel, a couple of moderately successful network marketing companies sold the original pre-IBM home computer. But once IBM captured the market, it spent millions in advertising and the network marketing venue quickly died.

What products and services don't work for network marketing?

Typically—with some notable exceptions—insurance, financial planning, and computer sales have not worked well as network marketing products. Why? Because the parts of the METS formula you need most in order to sell these products are *education* and *training*. Markets and products are changing rapidly; a salesperson has to spend so much time obtaining the knowledge necessary to provide education and training that it becomes impractical to have part-time distributors do it. These kinds of products require licenses for those who sell them, and often part-time distributors don't have enough time to invest in this kind of intense training.

> **On the Soapbox**
>
> For those of you who don't think I know about Primemerica and World Financial Group, I certainly do, and they are excellent examples of why I use the term "typically." Most of my "rules" have been proven wrong by one or two companies. If there were an exact formula for success, then anyone could follow that formula and be successful. Every successful company I know has made some of their own rules.

In summary, the products and services that work best in network marketing are usually those that require significant motivation and support, but do not require the distributor to spend excessive amounts of time *learning the product* or *educating and training the consumer*.

It's very important, as a company decides on its commission plan, that the decision-makers understand how much time a distributor needs to spend on motivation, education, training, and support (METS) to sell a product to the average consumer. The more time and energy it takes to make that sale, the more money needs to be paid directly to the salesperson. This, of course, means that less money is available for sales leader commissions.

II. Services

What about the *services* a network marketing company provides its network of distributors? Without helping its people to fulfill their needs for self-improvement, for increased self-esteem, for finding a way to do some good in the world, and at the same time meet their social needs, a company will struggle for success. The network marketing world is not an environment in which people can be treated as mere cogs in a machine—beings whose personal needs are irrelevant. If the company doesn't pay attention to the needs of its distributors, they'll go elsewhere—and the company will fail. The question many successful companies ask themselves when building their network marketing business is not only "What products should we sell?" but also "How can we change people's lives for the better?"

In fact, the services that a company provides are almost as important to some distributors as the money they make. In some ways, services are the great differentiator. What I mean by this is that, in the end, most products can be in some way duplicated by others. Commission plans can certainly be imitated. Therefore, the only real differentiation a company has to offer is often simply a matter of how much it helps the distributors grow, and how much it assists them in building their businesses.

Services come in two categories: *personal growth and development services*, and *business-building services*. Personal growth and development services include conventions, training and motivational seminars, and motivational tapes or CDs. Business-building services include retail consumer programs, web-based training, literature, training classes, and a consumer relations department.

III. Communications

Every successful network marketing company has had a "cause" or mission. Sometimes a mission revolves around a product, and sometimes it revolves around personal growth and development. More often than not, a company's mission is a combination of the two.

I've never seen a company succeed without successfully communicating a mission or purpose to its field force. But beware: some executives succumb to the temptation of embellishing the truth to make their mission sound better than it really is. They do so in order to appear more successful. The problem with using dishonesty as a way to bolster a company's mission is that if people act upon a false premise and then achieve notoriety and success, sooner or later Mike Wallace shows up at corporate headquarters, and the company's executives are looking guilty as sin, trying to explain that it was all a harmless misunderstanding.

In short: a company can prevent the possibility of misunderstanding by building a strong mission into its product line *and* corporate philosophy. This doesn't imply that the mission need be complex. The late Mary Kay Ash, for example, became world-renowned, both in and out of the industry, with the simple mission of *enriching women's lives*.

A company's leadership must communicate with its members on a regular basis. Communication gives direction, order, and enthusiasm. You no doubt remember that Ronald Reagan was called "the great communicator" by friend and foe alike. And he was. With a few simple words, he could re-energize his troops, lay out his agenda, or achieve whatever goal he had in mind. Unfortunately, most of us can't get all three networks and CNN to cover our speeches live, so we have to come up with a different way to communicate.

Every company needs a communications strategy. And every company's communications strategy must achieve several important goals:

1. A communications strategy must be inexpensive for the distributor.

2. The company message must reach distributors *regularly*. Motivation is like eating: you can't eat a big meal once a month and expect to remain full, so don't try to motivate distributors once a month and expect them to stay motivated!

3. Communications must encourage the distributorship to be active in their business.

4. Once the distributors establish a pattern in the way they communicate with the company, it's difficult to change. Therefore, a company must think its communications strategy through!

5. The communications strategy should integrate multiple forms of media so as to reach every level of your distributorship: newsletter; magazine; video; distributor kit; audio; CD; web site; web broadcasting and conference calls; local, regional, national, and international meetings and events.

6. Finally, the communications strategy must allow distributors to interact and communicate with their downlines.

A network marketing company's communications strategy is arguably more complex than that of traditional business because the sales force is more spread out and diverse, and because effective communication is essential to daily success.

Take the METS (Motivation, Education, Training, and Support) formula as an example: all of these functions are carried out via a company's communications strategy. In addition to multiple messages, the company is communicating with different audiences (consumers, prospects, distributors, and leaders) all over the country. And then there are scheduling issues: whereas some people can give two hours once a week, others will work twenty minutes every other day. The communications strategy needs to be flexible enough to effectively communicate with all of the distributors.

Finally, taking into account all of the above variables, a communications strategy must be easy to access and use. Until the advent of the Internet, this wasn't possible. Now, however, it's not only possible, but easy. *(Since I brought the Internet up, my company, InfoTrax, has created some great tools to help with this challenge. Don't forget to read Appendix E where I talk about WebMeeting—a great tool InfoTrax designed specifically to help networkers communicate inexpensively with each other over the Internet.)*

IV. Distributor commissions.

The last cornerstone is, of course, *distributor commissions*. Since the commission plan is the vehicle by which distributors receive their monetary rewards for the work they do, it needs to be reliable. It needs to ensure both distributor satisfaction and company profitability. Most importantly, the distributors need to perceive the company's commission plan as giving them a fair opportunity to seize their own destinies and meet their own financial goals.

Decisions about what kind of commission plan to follow should not be made until the company has made the basic decisions about its product line. The commission plan takes into account such issues as the socio-economic background of the distributors, how many full-time and part-time distributors there are, and the allocation of the commission money toward rewarding both selling product and managing sales. (Selling promotes stability; recruiting promotes growth.)

Another thing the commission plan will define is how much work a company will have to do to retain distributors and consumers, and how much work its distributors will do. In other words, in a "perfect" commission plan, the salespeople, sales leaders, and dream-builders do all the sales and marketing. In commission plans that fail to adequately compensate the leaders in one or more of these arenas, a company must counter this situation by taking on more of the load with their internal marketing and/or sales staff. In my experience, it's almost always better to let the distributors do the majority of the sales and marketing.

It's also very important that once a company sets up the basic structure of the commission plan, it not change the fundamental structure after the company has matured. Distributors build their downlines around the rules of a commission plan. Once the top distributors have spent years doing this, to have the company change the basic premise can undermine its best sales leaders.

How network marketing has changed

As I mentioned earlier, I've worked with the new network marketing companies of the past twenty years. These companies are very different from their predecessors, and it's important to understand how the industry has changed.

What has caused the differences between the network marketing company of the 1970s and one of today? In a word, *technology*. Five technologies in particular have revolutionized the industry.

Computers.

Fast, powerful, inexpensive computers have allowed companies to deal directly with all distributors, and increasingly with consumers as well. In the earlier days of the network marketing industry, top distributors were responsible for paying out earnings to their downlines. If a distributor failed to carry out his or her responsibilities, or if that distributor quit, chaos resulted.

Now, thanks to computers and software specifically designed to handle network marketing commission plans, a network marketing company can deal with all of its distributors from headquarters. A company can calculate, generate, and disburse distributor commissions in a timely manner. This approach is an enormous time-saver for distributors, who no longer have to perform these functions for their downlines. In the early 1980s, a traditional network marketing company conducted a survey asking their field leaders how much time they spent on administrative tasks. The average answer was sixty percent. Think of all of that time away from recruiting, selling, and training—what a waste!

Product Delivery.

Rapid package shipping. This is another technology that allows a company to deal directly with everyone. Distributors no longer have to maintain large inventories. Companies can have a more extensive product line. Distributors can recruit or sell to people living outside their local areas; they simply drop-ship orders to their consumers.

Communications.

The telecommunications revolution, particularly in terms of inexpensive long-distance telephone calls. Conference calls have replaced most weekly sales meetings. This means that distributors can recruit from anywhere. A company no longer starts in one region and slowly moves across the country or around the globe. Now distributors can be successful even if they don't know how to hold a meeting, because they can have their prospects listen in on conference calls hosted by others. Companies can afford to have 800-number ordering and even consumer service. This new ability can assist distributors in taking care of their consumers.

Videos and audiotapes.

Videos and audiotapes allow even relatively small companies to get their messages out in ways only major corporations could before. The use of videos for marketing and recruiting has greatly helped distributors to tell the company's story. It has also assisted in the explosion of remote sponsoring.

Internet.

The Internet will, I am convinced, have more effect on the industry than all of these technologies combined. I realize that as of this writing, the Internet hasn't yet realized its industry-wide potential—but it's starting to, and some companies have been very successful in using the Internet.

In June of 2002, the DSA released a survey of distributors from many companies. At that time, eighty-seven percent of these distributors had Internet access and used it in their businesses.

I know of several companies with sales in the hundreds of millions dollars annually, who enter between seventy and ninety percent of their orders via the Internet or automatic touchtone ordering. The distributors use this system because they choose to. Those who feel the least bit uncomfortable with technology are free to call an 800 number to place orders with live operators. Most, however, recognize and take advantage of the benefits of the newer technologies.

On the other hand, the Internet has reduced the window of opportunity for maximizing profit for a cutting-edge product. Everything moves faster in Internet time, and the length of time before a product becomes a commodity is constantly shrinking.

I believe that the core job of a company and its distributors is to motivate, educate, train, and support their consumers and downline. Technology allows distributors to accomplish their responsibilities on a level never before imagined. Technology, by allowing distributors to accomplish more in less time and to communicate more effectively to more people, is essential to new network marketing companies.

Some other effects of these technologies are:

- It's possible for a company to go international almost at once, even if they don't want it to!

- Companies no longer have to start out locally, building gradually over several years to a significant market presence. Most successful companies have spurts of meteoric growth. I worked with one company that signed up over a million distributors in less than three years! Such rapid growth creates enormous challenges for the company, but also creates enormous opportunities.

- Commission plans have become much more complex. Thirty years ago, commissions had to be simple enough for distributors to calculate by hand. Such is no longer the case.

Even more subtle changes have been caused by the technological revolution of the past twenty years. Now that a distributor no longer has to devote so much of his or her time to a single sale, the money a company spends on paying its distributors has gradually shifted from sales commissions to downline commissions.

Now that we've discussed the technology issues, let's look at the backbone of the business—*distributors*.

Understanding Multi-Level Commissions

Chapter Two

Key Topics

The five types of distributors 28
Sales commissions 33
Sales management commissions............................ 34
The effect of commission plans on distributor behavior 35
Why people join network marketing companies.............. 37
Rules of network marketing commission plans................ 39

Understanding Multi-Level Commissions

What do you need to know about distributors?

When I use the word "distributor," I mean anyone who has signed an application and, in most cases, purchased a sales kit. Most of the companies I have worked with are what I call "open-enrollment" network marketing companies. The numbers I deal with in this chapter are from open-enrollment companies. In this type of company, most people who become regular consumers of product sign up as "distributors." The other type of direct sales company is "barriers-to-signup." In this type of company, only those people who are serious about selling product become distributors. I discuss the differences between open-enrollment and barriers-to-signup in Chapter Eight.

If you have a network marketing company and you've signed up 100,000 typical distributors, the demographics are something like this: Between sixty and seventy percent *will not sponsor anyone*—not one! Of the remaining thirty percent who do sponsor someone, two-thirds sponsor five or fewer new distributors. Only the remaining third sponsor more than five new distributors.

$$\begin{array}{c} \text{60-70 percent sponsor no one} \\ \text{20-30 percent sponsor 1-5} \\ \underline{\text{10 percent sponsor 6+}} \\ =100 \text{ percent} \end{array}$$

I often hear a statistic batted around that the "average" distributor sponsors three people. This is incorrect. An average distributor sponsors one. (You derive the average by dividing the number of people who could sponsor someone by the number of people who are actually sponsored. In the above example, both numbers are 100,000 and the result is one – 100,000/100,000=1.)

Upon hearing this figure, people often inquire as to the best sponsoring rate I've ever seen. My answer? Slightly under forty percent—which means that even in the most productive companies in terms of sponsoring, more than sixty percent of their distributors are not sponsoring anyone.

Of those distributors who do sponsor someone, the average is between two and three. But that number will also mislead a company if they use it in their decision-making process. Why? Because, as the old story says, "If you have one leg in the stove and one leg in the icebox, on average you should be about the right temperature." If a company deals with average numbers in recruiting, it isn't addressing the fact that it's dealing with very different kinds of people. If the company wants to be successful, each group of people needs to have their specific needs dealt with. That makes much more sense than talking about the average needs of the organization. Instead, it's far better to talk about *the five types of distributors* when working through commission plan issues.

The five types of distributors

1. Consumers
2. Product evangelists
3. Salespeople
4. Sales leaders
5. Dream-builders

Consumers: This category includes most of the people who sign up, but don't recruit anyone else. Why did they sign up? For various reasons. Maybe they love the product and want a convenient way to purchase it at wholesale price. Or at the time, they really thought they might build the business, but later suffered rejection and changed their minds. Or perhaps the only reason they signed up in the first place was to get their brother-in-law out of the house so they could go back to watching the game!

Despite the fact that they signed an application, they're actually *consumers*. There is a good chance they want to purchase the product because they believe it helps them. It gives them more energy, or smoothes out their wrinkles, or whatever.

So what does a company do with these folks? If it treats them like salespeople, they'll almost certainly leave the organization. But if it treats them like *consumers*, maybe they'll stick around!

Consumers are vital to a company's success. If they weren't out there buying product from the distributors, there would be no company. The company must consider their interests in every decision it makes, including decisions relating to the commission plan. Consumer retention may be the biggest problem that most successful companies face.

Product evangelists. These people may or may not sponsor anyone. But in either case, recruiting other distributors is not the reason they're in the company. They love the product, they love to tell people about it, they want their friends and acquaintances to benefit from it, and they would recommend it even if they were not signed up. They simply don't want to invest a lot of time building a business or don't feel comfortable closing the sale.

Product evangelists can be a company's greatest asset if it can turn their contacts into distributors. The challenge in working with product evangelists is to keep them motivated and enthusiastic, and to work with them to turn their leads into new distributors.

We all know that the best kind of marketing is word-of-mouth—product evangelists prove it. They help a company's business. They are the "network" in "network marketing."

Salespeople. Salespeople usually earn between one thousand and several thousand dollars per month. These people are important because they sell product, they take care of consumers, they keep product evangelists happy, and they're the only ones who can do it. They do well in sales-oriented organizations. The product evangelist knows how to talk about the product and get others interested in it, but the salespeople know how to actually sell it, close, and follow up. They may or may not be strong in recruiting, but they know how to move product.

Sales leaders. The sales leaders, along with the salespeople, provide the backbone of a company's business. They hold the meetings, close the leads the product evangelists create, and keep the consumers happy and supplied with product. A good indicator of the health of a company is the stability of the income of the sales leaders. It's the sales leaders, in fact, who create stability for a company. If there's constant turnover, or if, after a reasonable amount of time working their business, they don't make enough money to justify the time and energy they put in, there is a problem.

One of the first recommendations I make to new clients is that they identify their salespeople and sales leaders and study the retention rate of these people. If it's high, a company's success is ensured. If it's low, the company has a problem it must solve quickly.

> A company doesn't have a lot of salespeople and sales leaders. If a company is doing $24 million a year in business, it likely has at least 30,000 consumers and product evangelists, but probably fewer than 1,000 salespeople, fewer than 100 sales leaders, and only a few dreambuilders.

Dream-builders. These distributors typically provide the leadership, passion, enthusiasm, and excitement for a company's mission. There are very few dream-builders in a company. They hold the big meetings; they "paint the dream" in the minds of everyone.

A company needs these people. They're the ones who understand, and can explain, the value proposition of the company in a way that people can understand it. I've never seen a company grow and prosper without at least one dream-builder, and most companies need several. Dream-builders can convince people, and best of all, they take the risks, open new markets, and communicate the company's mission.

I've listened to dozens of dream-builders speak. They have grand ideas. Dream-builders are the reason why a commission plan needs to provide a way to pay big earnings. Many people with this kind of personality, once they make enough money to support themselves, also need money to support their own businesses. Dream-builders spend a lot of money on their businesses. They fly around the country, sometimes the world. They hold meetings. Often, they have a staff. They print newsletters. Dream-builders are the ones who take a company into new markets. When a company opens a new country, the dream-builders are the ones who fly to that country to recruit distributors.

They're the ones who decide to reach out to different niche markets. All of these expenses are paid out of the pockets of the dream-builders.

Sometimes, if a company no longer wants the dream-builders to participate in what the company is doing, the company loses the boundless creative energy that dream-builders direct toward the company's success. They use that energy elsewhere. Often, when the dream-builders achieve the top level in a company, they slow down in building their organizations. Dream-builders are so goal-oriented that, when they no longer have goals to achieve, they lose their drive. The momentum of a company is generated by its dream-builders.

> *Anyone who likes a product can be a consumer or product evangelist, but the number of salespeople, sales leaders, and dream-builders is limited. I've never seen a company be successful without attracting and retaining a core of sales leaders and dream-builders.*

It's important to remember that just because a person is one of these types now, he or she isn't necessarily constrained from becoming another type. Several years ago, we did a study for a company about recruiting. Going into the study, we assumed that most distributors who had built good organizations had begun working hard immediately upon being sponsored. This was not the case. About sixty percent of the people who built organizations did get started within ninety days of the date they were sponsored, but forty percent didn't get started until later. Almost ten percent didn't start until more than a year after they were sponsored!

So which is most important—the consumer, the product evangelist, the salesperson, the sales leader, or the dream-builder? Every successful company knows it needs *all of these people*. Once the product evangelists and salespeople have brought people into the company, the dream-builders can reach down the tree, contact those new recruits who show promise, and raise up everyone who wants what the dream-builders have.

Everyone benefits from this kind of dynamic behavior within an organization. The recruiter benefits because his recruits make more, and so his income goes up accordingly. The recruit benefits because she finds a way to work toward her goals. The dream-builder benefits because he can pull together a unit of like-minded people to create the magic and achieve success. A company must maintain a balance among all three. It needs to allow all of these people to achieve their goals.

One of the big mistakes that companies make is to treat consumers and product evangelists like salespeople because they fail to do the research to sort them out. It's important for companies to make this differentiation because if a company treats consumers like salespeople, it won't be able to retain them. It requires researching and understanding each group, and it requires doing the traditional market research that virtually every other industry now performs. In the long term, if a company does not learn to break out, identify, and market to the specific needs of each of these types of distributors and market segments, then the company will ultimately suffer.

In addition to paying commissions, an example of a marketing strategy for each of these segments is:

1. Merchandise to consumers
2. Thank product evangelists
3. Support salespeople
4. Grow sales leaders
5. 5. Recognize dream-builders

A well-designed commission plan helps that to happen.

One question I often hear when discussing the five types of distributors is, "How do you design a commission plan around the needs of all of those people?" The answer is that you don't. It's important to remember that there's a difference between marketing strategy and commission plan design.

Yes, a company needs to build a marketing strategy around the five types of distributors, but, as a practical matter, commission plans are built around the dual considerations of *sales commissions* and *sales management commissions*. This is true because there are typically

Section One: What you need to know first

two major activities that companies want to encourage enough to pay distributors commissions for doing them. They are:

1. Selling product to consumers and servicing their needs.
2. Finding and managing salespeople to help them continue to sell product and grow.

Remember that it's illegal to pay commissions on *recruiting* in the United States. You can pay only on the *sale of product*. So a company doesn't pay commission for finding a salesperson; it pays commission only on the product that the salesperson sells.

Throughout this book, we'll judge the commission plans we examine in terms of how they pay sales commissions and how they pay sales management commissions. So let's talk about these two components of a commission plan.

Sales commissions

Sales commissions pay consumers, product evangelists, and salespeople. Most companies don't pay any sort of commissions to their consumers, but if the company or distributor decides to give a consumer a rebate on the product, that rebate comes out of the money reserved for sales commissions. In an open-enrollment company, sales commissions are difficult to design correctly because there is often a consumer in the following sponsorship situation:

Figure 2

When this happens, the commission plan needs to split the sales commission money between the product evangelist and the salesperson. In barriers-to-signup companies, the sales commission is easier to pay because the distributor gets the retail profit on any product he or she sells, thus earning that sales commission money directly. Because consumers and product evangelists don't usually sign up as working distributors, the challenge, in these types of companies, is figuring out how to pay the product evangelist for his or her role in the sale. (See Chapter Eight for more discussion of open enrollment versus barriers-to-signup companies.)

So a company must decide how much of its commission money to spend on sales commissions. Next, it must decide whether to use some of that money to give consumer rebates, and finally, create a strategy to ensure that if a product evangelist is involved in acquiring a consumer, that the product evangelist is properly compensated and the rest of the money flows up to the salesperson.

Sales management commissions

These commissions are much easier to design than sales commissions. This is because the needs of the sales leaders and dream-builders are similar. Therefore, unlike sales commissions where a lot of time is spent worrying about how to pay the right person, with sales management commissions the biggest worry is creating consistency in the payout.

Consistency is the number-one rule of the game in sales management commissions. If a sales leader has $200,000 of downline volume three months in a row, but the checks that leader receives for each of the three months are $20,000, $5,000, and $14,000, the company has a problem. It does happen, and it's not a pretty sight. Sales leader commissions need to be predictable.

> *Each month, a distributor must become more confident that he can predict the amount of his commission check. Nothing is worse than an unpredictable commission plan!*

The other important item is that the qualifications to achieve higher ranks need to build on each other and remain consistent. For example, commission qualifications should not reward building deep for the first few ranks and then switch to reward building wide.

The effect of commission plans on distributor behavior

There is a wide range of multi-level commission plans. Some of these plans are designed to pay relatively high commissions to the person actually selling the product, and less money in "downline commissions." In other companies, the commissions focus is more on downline commissions and less on commissions to the person selling the product. I'm going to discuss the differences between the two, and the pros and consof each.

In a sales-oriented network marketing company, it's possible for distributors to make good money simply by selling product. Suppose, for example, that at one company selling cosmetics, distributors earn fifteen to twenty percent on product they sell. By offering a reasonably high percentage, that particular company encourages its distributors to build a good retail sales business. However, in a true direct sales company, the commission would more likely be in the forty percent range. So why have so many companies of the last twenty years chosen network marketing instead of direct sales as their method of product distribution?

There are two reasons. One is that sales alone, with no recruiting, leads to a lack of growth. Companies have found that taking on the responsibility of recruiting enough distributors nationwide to keep the company growing has become too difficult and expensive to handle internally. It's easier and more effective to assign that responsibility to the distributors. For example in 2001, Avon, one of the oldest and most successful direct sales companies, converted to a multi-level commission plan.

The other reason is that the prospect of earning downline commissions in addition to sales commissions is very powerful. Even for successful salespeople who are not sure they can build a large downline, there are two benefits. One is the fact that a multi-level commission plan can create a group of paid referral agents to refer business to the distributor. The second benefit is the possibility of one of these referral agents building a big business is very attractive.

But some network marketing companies have also become unbalanced in the other direction. There have been companies with tens of thousands of distributors who are consistently recruiting new distributors, but who never get around to selling any product. These companies create a big problem for themselves, and there have been several over the last few years. Companies with a high percentage of downline commissions, but little, if any, sales commissions, have sometimes grown quickly, but then had difficulty sustaining their momentum. This is because all of these distributors have little incentive to sell much product because they only may make a small percentage on product sales and it isn't worth the time. If you have an entire company doing this, all you have is a huge downline.

The important thing is to create a commission plan that encourages and compensates the activities a company wants its distributors to perform. For most companies, this means that distributors should be encouraged to spend a significant amount of time in both recruiting and selling, but a company must design its commission plan to elicit the balance it believes is best.

Obviously, the type of commission plan a company designs has a strong influence on how distributors work to build their business. As you read this book, keep in mind what kind of *balance* between sales commissions and sales management commissions you think is appropriate.

In a traditional sales organization, as I pointed out earlier, the role of a salesperson is to sell product, period. It isn't the responsibility of the salesperson to bring in new people to perform this task. In a network marketing organization, however, a distributor has the dual responsibility of both selling and recruiting. When a company chooses a commission plan, it must be sure the plan rewards the balance of distributor activities it believes is correct.

One last thought. Recruiting exists to build the capacity for sales—to create the infrastructure. With that in place, a company must promote sales, because that's what brings in the money. The more a company promotes recruiting, the faster its sales force grows. But that growing sales force is only a *potential* means to increase sales; no one earns any money if the distributors aren't selling. You may have heard the old expression about someone who is "too busy sawing to sharpen the saw." Or in this case, sometimes companies are "too busy recruiting to stop and sell the product."

Why people join network marketing companies

What are people looking for when they join network marketing companies? Why do they choose this route to help achieve their goals rather than looking for another traditional job with a company that offers a regular salary and a certain amount of stability and predictability?

I've found three main reasons why people make such a choice.

- Community needs
- Income needs
- Self-improvement

The first has to do with **community needs**. Our society no longer offers many of the forums in our communities that once gave people a sense of belonging, a sense of purpose. To a large degree, our society has lost its interpersonal connections. Town meetings and other community events no longer occur to create a sense of community. The workplace is volatile, the population is mobile, the culture places less emphasis on the family, and many have lost contact with the religious structures that used to give people that all-important feeling of being part of something valuable. If you don't belong to a church where you can feel at home, if your employer seems ready to downsize you out the door at any moment, if you've moved hundreds of miles away from your home community, if you don't have a feeling of being connected—well, you see what I mean. It's possible to live in a huge city, with millions of inhabitants, and still feel isolated. In today's mobile society, we're actually a tribal people without tribes.

What does all this have to do with network marketing companies? A great deal, actually. If you're a member of a network marketing organization, you belong. You have a place. You connect with your consumers, with your downline, with your mentors in the business. You're helping people to purchase a product or a service that will improve their lives. You attend conventions and motivational seminars that help you to improve as a person. You're on the team. In a society such as ours, in which people often find themselves alone and lonely in the midst of the crowd, belonging to a group can give meaning and purpose to an otherwise unfocused life.

The second reason for becoming involved in a network marketing enterprise has to do with ***income needs***. In today's volatile workplace, people simply don't have the job security that workers once enjoyed. Today's employees tend to change employers every few years. Even if you do have fairly stable employment, the chances are that your income is far less than you feel you need or deserve.

Also, people view the money they earn from a network marketing company as different from the pay they receive from a regular employer. Why? If you're an employee of Acme Widgets, the only way for you to receive a promotion may be for someone to die or quit. It doesn't matter how good you are or how hard you work. But in network marketing, you have a great deal of control over what you make. You're motivated not only by what you're making now, but by your potential earnings. And no one can stop you.

What often makes people worried and depressed is not hard work or responsibility, but lack of control over their own lives. Because so many workers from all levels—blue-collar, pink-collar, middle management, executive—are feeling manipulated and shuffled around at work, they eventually decide to take charge of their own destinies and control their own incomes.

The way to achieve this goal is often by joining a network marketing organization, which offers people the chance to achieve whatever they're willing to work for. In network marketing, an individual may reach a level of income he or she could not achieve in the traditional workplace while lacking the degrees or the years of experience required. A conscientious distributor can see a genuine relationship between the effort put forth and the financial reward received.

The third reason people join network marketing organizations is for ***self-improvement***. A traditional company usually trains employees only in what they must know to be able to provide the services the company needs from them. But many people have a need for personal growth far beyond cursory job training. Network marketing organizations, with their motivational rallies, training tapes and seminars, and mentoring structures, fill that need. A Mary Kay beauty consultant, for instance, may not become rich beyond her wildest dreams. But at sales meetings she receives, for free, the same kind of training normally only available to corporate managers; she gains experience in working with people; and she grows in confidence and skill level. She also gains control over her work environment. The same is true of the experience many distributors have with the top network marketing companies, whose executives understand how vital this need is among those who sign up.

Network marketing companies not only sell the product; they also give their people the motivation to change and improve. A distributor might find himself or herself learning and growing for the first time since leaving school. A network marketing organization might say to its people, "Our mission is to make you more than you are. Our commitment to you extends beyond the products we sell."

If you've spent much time browsing the shelves in bookstores, you know that a large percentage of the non-fiction books for sale are in the area of self-improvement. Millions of people in today's world have an overwhelming need to make themselves more than they are now—not just in terms of income, but in terms of confidence, ability, spirituality, physical condition, you name it. An organization that makes it a priority to help its members achieve these goals has a powerful appeal.

Rules of network marketing commission plans

Now that we've discussed the three reasons people join network marketing companies, let's talk about the rules that cause network marketing commission plans to succeed. Over the years, I've developed three rules that I believe apply to successful commission plans. These three rules are:

1. The stability of a company is a function of the number of $500 commissions it pays out each month.[1]
2. The excitement about a company is based on the ability to earn a $50,000 commission.

---

[1] Obviously these numbers are approximations, but they give you the idea.

3. Commission plans are self-fulfilling prophecies.

Rule #1 - Stability. *The stability of a company is a function of the number of $500 commissions it pays out each month.* This rule refers to salespeople. This is important because distributor retention is much higher when distributors are earning $500 a month than when distributors are earning less than $100 a month. There is not an exact number, and the number is different for each company. However, there always seems to be a point in the few hundred dollar range (I say $500 because it's a good round number) where retention takes a dramatic turn upward. I was struck by a speech made in a convention many years ago. The statement was to the effect that "The difference between the life a person is leading and the life he wants to lead is usually a few hundred dollars a month."

The income a person makes as a distributor for a network marketing company is often a second income, on top of a full-time job. Suppose that your "day job" isn't necessarily something you want to give up, but you're not satisfied with the level of income it produces, or with the challenge it presents, or with the level of growth it offers. How much additional income will it take to keep you involved in a second income-producing effort? It will have to be worth the free time you'll have to sacrifice. You might, for example, wind up going to a sales meeting or delivering products rather than watching the playoff game for (insert sport of your choice here) or browsing the Internet or reading a good book. For most people, the answer to "How much will it take?" currently seems to be around $500 a month.

Why that amount? Because our society demands that whatever a person earns on the job should go to the family—car payments, mortgage, the children's education—but often the money earned through a side business is that person's *own* money. (Some people call it "mad money".) That extra few hundred a month means that now people can achieve what they want. They may not be able to believe they could earn ten times what they're making now, but they may be able to visualize a life of making ten to fifteen percent more. The extra money can let them have the extras they want without having to fight the family budget for it. That ability makes a huge difference to network marketing because it motivates people to work as distributors and to stick with the company.

So for these distributors, whose primary motivation is additional income, this "extra" $500 a month will keep them working for a company. The commission plan should enable the distributors to reach this level as quickly as possible. If they work and struggle for many months without earning more than a few $50 or $100 commissions, they often quit. That small additional income isn't worth the time and effort required to earn it. To retain distributors, the company needs a commission plan that brings those distributors who are committed to this critical mass of approximately $500 as soon as possible. How does a company design a plan to get them to $500 as quickly as possible? By making sure that after they've proven they're serious by moving past the product evangelist role to the salesperson role, the percentage they earn on their downline increases.

For example, if the plan pays out five percent on downline sales, a distributor needs $10,000 in sales to earn $500. But if the commission plan lets distributors make twenty percent instead of only five percent on downline sales, they can start bringing in $500 a month with only $2,500 in sales.

Figure 3

Obviously, many more people can achieve this level of sales than can reach $10,000. That means that more people will be motivated to continue because they've reached a level of additional income that's meaningful to them.

Rule #2 - Excitement. *The excitement about a company is based on the ability to earn $50,000 commissions.* Allowing people to make $500 a month isn't all a company has to think about. Many people become involved with network marketing companies because they have a big dream. Some people can see themselves making a whole lot of money, and that's what they want to do when they sign up as a distributor. A commission plan needs to allow for the dream-builders as well as for the people who only want a few hundred extra dollars each month.

If dream-builders believe that others are achieving a large income through a company—if they believe that working as a distributor for Company X will give them financial independence—they'll be excited about becoming distributors, and they'll work hard. What the company must avoid is misleading them. We all know that only a small percentage of distributors in this industry ever become rich, but it isn't fair to use a bait-and-switch commission plan. If a company wants to attract the dream-builders—and successful companies have at least a few of them—it must be *possible* for a distributor to achieve the dream if he or she works the business. Once the dream-builders discover that it isn't possible to get where the company told them they could go by means of a commission plan, they're gone.

So what is a "whole lot of money"? I use $50,000 a month, but is that the amount it takes to guarantee success? I know of very successful companies that send out monthly commission checks in the hundreds of thousands of dollars. I also know of very successful companies that could never send out a single commission check that would even come close to my number of $50,000. But like I said, they're successful, so which is right?

To some extent, this is one of the great unanswerable questions. However, we can answer some portions of it. If a company shows Ferraris, million-dollar mansions, stretch limousines, and private jets in their literature, but the maximum that top distributors can earn is $10,000 a month, the company has a problem. Companies need to set expectations in line with their earnings potential. The second issue is that disclosure is important. Distributors need to know what a commission plan can possibly pay. And last of all, it's important for companies to remember what work they expect distributors to do for the commissions they earn, and make sure that these commissions are in line with the work expected.

Rule #3 - Self-Fulfilling Prophecy. *Commission plans are self-fulfilling prophecies.* I say this because people can't work a plan they don't believe in. The company and its sales leaders have to believe in the commission plan it implements. (A mediocre plan that creates excitement, and therefore sales, is better than a great plan that creates neither.) Because the fact of the matter is, if a company is paying out forty percent in commissions and, because the distributors believe in the plan, they sell $1,000,000 in product, $400,000 will get paid out. The company is better off than if they had a "better" plan that that the distributors didn't like and only generated $100,000 in sales, and hence paid only $40,000 in commissions. I learned this lesson years ago – never recommend a plan the sales leaders hate. You will look bad because there will be no sales and your plan will be blamed. I did, I was, and it was. It was not a pleasant experience!

> *A mediocre plan that generates lots of excitement, and sales, is better than a great plan that generates neither. Of course, the challenge is creating a plan that generates excitement and is well designed.*

Do all network marketing companies need the same balance between sales and sales management? No. That's one reason there is no one perfect commission plan. In Chapter Three, I am going to talk about the steps to designing a commission plan. Then in Section Two, in order to understand the other significant aspects of a commission plan, we'll look at the major components of the commission plan itself: *commissions, rules,* and *structures*. I'll be referring to these concepts throughout this book, so you need to read this next section carefully if you don't already have a thorough understanding of these components.

Understanding Multi-Level Commissions

Chapter Three

Key Topics

Five steps to a commission plan design 48

Understanding Multi-Level Commissions

Chapter Three: Where do you begin?

Although this is a book about understanding commissions, it's not a book about commission plan design. However, I decided to include one chapter that talks about the basics of putting a plan together. I do a great deal of consulting for network marketing companies. When I begin working with the management team for a company, sometimes they say to me, "What is the world's best commission plan?"

This question is an impossible one to answer, of course. In this chapter, I'll explain just why it's impossible as stated. Then we'll look at the issues you need to deal with in creating the perfect commission plan *for your company*.

No set law defines what you can do as a network marketing company. There are a few laws telling you what you *can't* do, and there are a few landmark legal cases as examples of what not to do. But you don't start out with a clear list of regulations, as you would in the insurance business. When you create your own business, you have a great deal of freedom—and therefore a great deal of responsibility. One of your

> **Economic dynamics and commission plans**
>
> One successful company touts the fact that it has an extraordinary number of doctors and lawyers as distributors. The reason is the fact that their top distributors can make as much a $500,000 per month.
>
> There's a concept that makes sense. If your top distributors make $20,000 per month, you won't get a lot of doctors and lawyers. They can earn that much in their current occupation. It takes a lot more money than that to turn these people's heads.
>
> Can you be successful if your top earners make $20,000 per month? Many companies have. But if your product is of interest only to people in the top socio-economic stratum of society, you need distributors in that stratum. In that case, your top earners need to make far more.

most important responsibilities is to design a commission plan that works *for your company*.

The questions you need to ask yourself as you begin designing a commission plan revolve around the theme of "What do I want my company to do?" Like any entrepreneur hoping to build a successful business, you need to be very clear on what you want your company to achieve and how you want your company to operate in order to meet that goal.

The commission plan you develop and implement needs to reflect your *values* and *beliefs*. What another network marketing executive considers acceptable might not be what you consider acceptable. What do you believe, and what do people with your same values believe? Those beliefs must guide and control your company. You must develop a commission plan that encourages distributors to behave in such a way that fosters and supports those beliefs.

Five steps to a commission plan design

As with any complex question, it's best to break it down into smaller steps and tackle them one at a time. These are the five steps to commission plan design:

1. Establish your company's mission, product and service strategy, and intellectual distribution strategy.

2. Decide what percentage of your product price you want to pay out in commissions.

3. Divide your commission payout between sales commissions and sales management commissions.

4. Decide which commissions and qualification methods to use.

5. Create an ongoing series of contests and incentives targeted at the five types of distributors that fit with the commission plan you created.

If this sounds like a great oversimplification, it is. In fact, a friend of mine, Winston Lambert, put it best when he said, "Designing a commission plan is like playing chess against a grand master—unfortunately, some people treat it like they're playing tic-tac-toe."

> **Commission plans: Understanding the Game Board.**
>
> In a way, a commission plan is like learning to play chess. It seems easy at first; all you have to do is learn what each piece can do. The bishop can move diagonally, the knight can jump over another piece and then scoot over a square, the queen can move in any direction, and so forth. But then when you start playing actual games, you find out that you have to think about a whole lot more than that. Are you overlooking an opportunity to capture your opponent's powerful queen? What is likely to happen three moves from now, or six moves from now? Is your king open to checkmate?

So now that I've given you the steps, let's review them one at a time.

1. **Establish your company's mission, product and service strategy, and intellectual distribution strategy.** I can't stress enough the importance of knowing these things before a company embarks on designing its commission plan. As we discussed earlier, your company's mission creates a framework for what products your company can sell and what it can't sell. Knowing your product and service strategy will allow you to make the all-important decisions about pricing and commission percentages. And if you don't know how much of a role you expect your distributors to play in your intellectual distribution strategy, it will be very difficult to decide how much of a sales commission they need to earn for fulfilling that role. One of the big questions companies have to ask themselves is whether they're going to adopt an open-enrollment or barrier-to-signup strategy. I discuss this issue in depth in Chapter Eight. However, a commission plan should naturally flow from the company's mission and strategies.

Understanding Multi-Level Commissions

2. **Decide what percentage of your product price you want to pay out in commissions.** It's hard to overstate the importance of this step. In the end, one of the most important factors as to whether or not your company will be successful is—will consumers who are not earning commissions, and never plan to earn commissions, buy your product? It's very important that the consumers believe they're getting value for their money. If you ask distributors what percentage a company should pay in commission, many of them will say, "The more the better." Believe me, I have asked. So is that true? Is more always better? I argue that it's not, and here's why. Let's take it to the extreme. If a company pays out 99.99% commissions on a product that costs $1.00 to produce, that product will sell for $1,000.00. You can see the problem. No one is going to buy a product priced that high, so the distributors' income from selling it will be zero. It's an interesting concept.

Actually, an economist who advised President Ronald Reagan created a theory about income tax rates that showed the same thing. Congress seemed to think that if it kept raising taxes, the government would keep getting more revenue. However, Dr. Arthur Laffer showed that when the tax rate reached approximately thirty percent, tax revenue would actually start to decline because people no longer had an incentive to work. So you can see from Figure 4

Figure 4

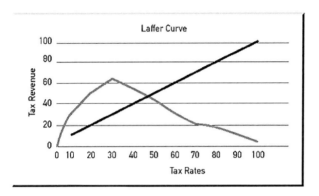

that if the tax rate is zero percent the government receives zero revenue, but if the tax rate is 100 percent, the government also receives zero revenue. So the optimum tax rate for the government to receive the maximum amount of tax revenue is about thirty percent. The same is true of commission percentages. If the commission percentage is zero percent, the distributors' earnings are zero. If the commission percentage is 99.9999%, the distributors' earnings will also probably be zero. So what is the optimum percentage? It is **the percentage where a distributor earns the most total overall commissions because the product has not started to price itself out of the market, and hence, sales have not started to decline**. Each product line is different, and I don't know that anyone has done the research in our industry that Dr. Laffer did about income taxes, but history can give us a good indication. If you look over the last twenty years at successful companies, most of them pay between thirty-five and fifty percent in commissions. Now obviously, if a company is selling long-distance service, they can't pay anywhere near that kind of percentage. Or if a product requires a lot of training, they may pay more and still be successful. I am simply talking about the averages.

3. **3. Divide your commission payout between sales commissions and sales management commissions.** We talked about this a little in Chapter Two. There are basically

five types of distributors, all with different needs. These differing needs dictate the need for a somewhat complex marketing and communications strategy on the part of most network marketing companies. One of the most fascinating aspects of network marketing is that companies don't have only one type of relationship with their distributors. Distributors are their consumers, sales forces, and sales management, just to name a few. InfoTrax once conducted a research project showing that distributors often assume all of those roles during a single consumer service phone call to the company. Luckily, the complexity of dealing with the five types of distributors is, to a large extent, confined to marketing, communications, contests, and incentives. Commissions, by and large, deal entirely with activities for which companies want to create permanent compensation: selling product, and managing the people who sell product.

Once companies determine the total amount available for commissions, they need to decide how much is going to be paid to the person(s) involved in selling the product and how much is going to be paid to the people involved in sales management. Let's start with sales management. Over the last few years, more and more commission revenue has moved to the sales management side. In fact, in some companies, it's hard to see that any money is set aside for the salesperson.

In this area, we asked the same question about overall commission percentage of the sales leaders that we asked the salespeople: "What percentage should be paid for the sales leadership?" Some of them say, "Most or all of it." However, if you're trying to recruit people only to sell product and none of the commission amount is set aside for them, how many salespeople are you going to recruit? The answer is, obviously, none. The sales leader earns more when he has people selling more product, but no one wants to be sponsored to sell product for nothing.

> Companies sometimes want to pay people for recruiting salespeople, but it's illegal in the USA and many other countries. Many have thought they have found a tricky way around the laws, and often they get away with it for a while, but when they become successful enough, they get caught.

What is a reasonable split between sales commissions and sales management commissions? As far as I know, no one has done extensive research, but over the last twenty years, the successful companies seem to break it down like this:

Figure 5

Network Marketing Companies	
Sales	50 - 60%
Sales management	50 - 40%
Total	100%

Party Plan Companies	
Sales	60 - 75%
Sales management	40 - 25%
Total	100%

Again, these are rough averages, which don't take into account the retail profit of network marketing companies. Also, there are many exceptions, and some plans do not lend themselves to being broken down in this fashion. I discuss these issues in the section on commission plans.

4. Decide which commissions and qualification methods to use. There are two major categories of commission plans. They are:

a. Structured plans, which include binary and matrix

b. Unstructured plans, which are basically everything else

Structured plans limit the number of first-level distributors a person can sponsor. This means that the downline is "structured." Additionally, some structured plans do allow a distributor to have more than one position in the tree. I will discuss this in detail later. The two main variations of structured plans are:

a. **Matrix** – This type of plan has been around since the early 1980s. These plans are based on the premise that the organization of the downline is key factor in a company. So they limit how many first-level distributors any one distributor can have in order to force the distributor tree to be built according to a certain structure. They typically use a unilevel payout, but there are many payout variations.

b. **Binary** – This plan only allows a distributor to have two first level distributors in their organization, so the downline is a type of matrix; hence, we use the computer term "binary tree" to describe the plan. The payout in a binary plan is unlike anything done before. It truly forms a class by itself.

Unstructured plans are basically all other types of plans, and they tend to use between two and five commissions types in their commission plan. The term "unstructured" means that they don't limit the number of first levels a distributor can have. However, many companies do have requirements to achieve ranks in the commission plan, such as having a certain number of first-level distributors of a certain rank.

The basic commission types used are the same between structured and unstructured plans. Certain questions often come up when we start talking about which commission plan to use and which commission types to use. One of the most frequent questions is "Why do companies use more than one commission type?" A very good question. Once the company has decided on the percentage split between sales commissions and sales management commissions, then it must decide how to pay them. Here is the challenge. When you're trying to pay sales commissions, you're trying to accumulate the commissions to the one or two people who actually were involved in the sale. So in this case, the company is trying to pay very targeted commissions.

How do they do that? Well, you have to make some assumptions. If this is the first person the sponsor has brought into the business, you have to assume that the sponsor is still being trained. You should probably make that assumption even if this is his second or even third person sponsored. So, the computer searches upline until it finds someone who meets the criteria the company has defined and pays that person the commission. The company can create rules to split the commission between multiple people in certain cases or pay it all to one person in other cases. But in the case of sales commissions, you typically use a commission type that allows the entire sales commission to be targeted to one or two individuals. *The important concept in sales commissions is that once someone has advanced from consumer through product evangelist to salesperson, they receive the majority of sales commissions from the product sold to the consumers and product evangelists in their organization*

> **When you're trying to pay sales commissions, you're trying to accumulate the commissions to the one or two people who actually were involved in the sale.**

Sales management commissions, on the other hand, are a completely different animal. Sales management is typically split between a couple of sales leaders and one or two dream-builders. So for sales management commissions, you are looking for a type of commission that spreads the wealth rather than targets earnings. Why? Because the downside to a type of commission that targets earnings is that one day it may target them to one person and away from someone else. The key to successful sales management commissions is consistency. As a sales leader or dream-builder builds their downline, their earnings should grow in relation to their downline volume, until sales volume starts moving out of their payline. For sales management commissions, the goal is to spread the commissions out between several sales leaders.

> *For sales management commissions, the goal is to spread the commissions out between several sales leaders.*

Typically, then, a company needs at least two types of commissions: one to take care of the basic needs of sales commissions, and one to take care of sales management. On top of that, companies like to encourage certain specific behaviors, and that canadd additional commission types to the plan. This is why a company can have up to five or more commission types in a plan.

In my discussion of sales commissions, I mentioned that the company had to create rules in order to ensure that the sales commission goes to the person or persons they want to pay. This brings us to the issue of qualification rules. People often have the mistaken belief that the *commission type* determines the success or failure of a plan. While the commission types certainly play a major role, the *qualification rules* to become a distributor, maintain a distributorship, and qualify for commissions, are at least as important in determining the success or failure of a commission plan. Why?

The qualification rules are the only means the computer has to sort out consumers, product evangelists, salespeople, sales leaders, and dream-builders. If these rules do not reflect reality, then people are paid for jobs they're not performing, and vice versa.

Let me give you an example. Let's talk about group qualification in most plans. What happens if group qualification is set too high? Distributors must purchase product that they can't sell and store it in their garages in order to meet the excessive requirements. Hence the term "garage qualified." But what if the group qualification is set far too low? Traditional group qualifications of $1,000-$3,0000 per month are relatively common, but lately we're seeing some companies with group qualification requirements of $200 with the same type of plan.

So what's the problem with that? An upline sales leader makes five percent on the group volume of five generations in his organization. In a traditional company, that yields $50-$150. In the company with the lower requirements, that ends up to be only $10. An even bigger problem is the fact that distributors who meet the group qualification requirements, instead of earning $200-$500 per month in the traditional plan, are now only earning $40 but are expected to fulfill the same roles as when they made more money.

This is but one example of how qualification rules make the plan. Don't ever let yourself fall into the trap of deciding on a plan, calculating what you would earn, or comparing one plan with another without understanding all of the qualifications.

> **On the Soapbox**
>
> It's extremely important, as you work through steps to commission plan design, that you base them on some realities rather than just throwing something together. Once you make your commission plan, you need to be prepared to stick to the basic structure forever. One of the saddest and most frustrating things that I see, happens when a distributor works for five or ten years or more to build a downline organization around the commission plan defined by the company, only to have the company change the commission plan to reward a completely different structure of organization. All of that distributor's hard work goes to waste.

5. **Create an ongoing series of contests and Incentives targeted at the five types of distributors that fit with the type of commission plan you created.** This is an important issue, but I won't spend much time on it in this book. I just want to make two important points:

    a. The commission plan gives people *financial incentive* to stay involved in a company. *The reasons* people stay involved are considerably more complex. In Chapter Two, I talked about the fact that there are three reasons that distributors join companies – community needs, income needs, and self-improvement. The products and services of the company also play a key role in distributor loyalty. I have never seen a company thrive and prosper over the long term that did not adequately address all of these aspects.

    b. Commission plans should be *consistent*. Contests and incentives should vary, should build on each other, and should support the plan. They provide the fun of the business. Contests help people pay their way to conventions, pay their way on cruises, and so on. It's literally a way to get everyone involved.

In the next section of the book, we're going to discuss in depth the building blocks of a commission plan. This discussion will give us the background for the final section of the book: a look at standard commission plan types and the pros and cons of each.

Section Two: The Building Blocks

In Section Two, my main goal is to help you to understand the components that make up every commission plan. The chapters for Section Two are as follows:

Chapter 4: Commissions. I will review the strengths and weaknesses of each commission type and also explain how you can use each type of commission to achieve a specific objective in commission plan design. Commissions alone do not define the commission plan, but they're certainly of great importance to your distributors! I'll go into details about the various types of commissions in Chapter Four.

Chapter 5: Rules. Rules define the qualifications a distributor must meet in order to be paid commissions on downline activity. They also specify the criteria for earning other awards or benefits from the company. For example, do you expect a new distributor to purchase a kit on signup? Do you require them to purchase a demonstration kit? How many months can a distributor go without results before losing the distributorship or being reduced in rank? Does the company require a distributor to take certain training classes before moving up in rank? How much must a distributor sell each month to remain qualified at the current level? What are the most common qualifications?

Chapter 6: Structure. The term "structure" refers to the overall organization a distributor's downline must have in order for him to receive certain commission payments: in other words, the specific set of rules in a commission plan that determines where people must be placed in the organization. How do distributors build downlines? What will the downline look like as the company grows? How effective will the organization be in terms of motivation, payout, distribution, and so on?

Some commission plans are very structure-oriented. The commission plan defines what the organization will look like: for example, a distributor may be allowed to build his business by personally sponsoring only three distributors. Other commission plans simply require that a distributor do certain things without demanding a specific structure.

Chapter 7: Miscellaneous commissions. These are commissions that companies use to supplement the "big four" commissions that make up the majority of commission plans. These commissions are matching commissions, automobile commissions, fast start commissions, and incentives.

Chapter 8: Operational issues. In Chapter Eight, I discuss the operational issues that all network marketing companies must address. They may not deal directly with the nuts and bolts of the company's commission plan, but the decisions the company makes regarding these issues have a direct impact on the company's commission plan.

Chapter Four

Key Topics

Overview 61
Level commissions 62
  Pros and Cons: Strengths of level commissions 67
  Challenges inherent with level commissions 67
  Related Issue... 68
Differential commissions 75
  Pros and Cons: Differential commission strong points........ 80
  Weaknesses of differential commissions 81
  Related Issues.. 81
Single-level commissions 82
  Pros and Cons: Benefits of single-level commissions 84
  Disadvantages of single-level payout 84
  Summary 85
Pool commissions 85
  Pros and Cons: Pros of a pool commission 88
  Disadvantages of a pool commission........................ 88
  Summary 88
Conclusion... 88

Understanding Multi-Level Commissions

What are the types of commissions that help define commission plans?

Overview

Over the years, commission plans have changed drastically. By and large, these changes have come about because of technology. Because few companies had computers thirty years ago, plans had to be simple enough that distributors could calculate commissions by hand. Once computers took over this task, commission plans became more complex.

With one exception, the basic types of commissions that companies pay have remained the same. **There are only two types of multi-level commissions: *level commissions* and *differential commissions*.** These types can pay a commission to multiple distributors on the same dollar of sales under a defined set of rules. The other two types of commissions are **single-level commissions**, which, as its name denotes, means that the entire commission amount goes to a single person, and **pool commissions,** in which an amount of money is put into a pool and divided up among those who qualify. I was startled to realize that there were only four types of commissions! After all, my company has programmed hundreds of different commission plans, and no two are exactly the same. It seems strange. But it gets stranger. The vast majority of network marketing commissions are paid as either level commissions or differential commissions. Pool and single-level commissions are typically used as "finishing touch" commissions. There are some exceptions, but they generally account for a small percentage of the overall payout of a company.

Most modern commission plans contain a combination of multiple commission types. They're set up this way because under normal conditions no single commission type can simultaneously target earnings to the salesperson and also spread commissions out among several sales leaders and dream-builders. For each commission type, I'll discuss how it functions, what the pros and cons are, and what distributor activities it rewards. My goal is to give an objective description of each commission type in terms of how it affects the distributors and the companies. It's not my goal to sell you on one type or another. As you read the following sections about the different commission types, you'll notice that I give a general overview and then go into more detail about each type.

Note: Appendix D gives you sample payout exercises for level and differential commissions that you can work through. You might find it helpful to work through the examples as you read these sections.

Level commissions

Overview: The *level* commission is the most common type of commission found in network marketing. Of all the companies I've worked with over the last twenty years, virtually every one of them, except binaries, had at least one level commission in their plan. The term "multi-level marketing" probably originated from this type of commission.

A level commission is a spread-the-wealth tool. Its goal is to ensure that distributors are always paid on their downline. It also tends to have a very smooth, stable line of earnings growth; in other words, it grows slowly and steadily over time. As its name denotes, this commission pays the distributor a percentage on a certain number of levels of his or her downline.

There are many variations of this commission. Some of those variations are called *unilevel, generation*, and *matching* commissions. These are just a few of the many usages of this most common commission type.

Usage: The strength of the level commission is that it builds long-term financial stability. The drawback is that it doesn't allow a company to target commissions to any specific type of distributor.

As a result, the role of level commissions in paying salespeople is fairly limited. In order to be part of a successful commission strategy for salespeople, it needs to be used in conjunction with other commission types.

The fact that it can create very stable earnings has meant that a level commission paid on group volume, often referred to as a generation commission, is the de facto standard for paying sales management commissions. Many other methods have been tried and only a couple have the potential to work as well as a generation commission

The Details: A level commission is defined as one that pays a fixed percentage on a fixed number of levels of a distributor's genealogy. A distributor who qualifies for a level commission is paid on the volume that occurs within the defined number of levels. There's typically no limit to the amount of volume a distributor can receive commission on, nor are commissions blocked if someone in that person's downline achieves a higher rank. (Level commissions are referred to as "non-blocking commissions." We'll talk about blocking commissions in the section on differential commissions.)

Figure 6

1-Star	2-Star	3-Star	
5%	5%	5%	1st Level
5%	5%	5%	2nd Level
5%	5%	5%	3rd Level
	5%	5%	4th Level
		5%	5th Level

Almost any level commission offered by any company has a chart that looks like the one in Figure 6. What does it mean? Look at the column labeled "1-Star." The chart tells you that a distributor who has achieved the rank of 1-Star is qualified to receive five percent commissions on sales generated on the first three levels of distributors. The 1-Star will be paid that commission, regardless of the ranks achieved by any downline distributors.

Now look at the second column. The chart tells you that distributors who achieve the rank of 2-Star earn five percent commissions on sales generated on four levels of sponsorship. The third column tells you that distributors who achieve the rank of 3-Star earn five percent commissions on five levels of sponsorship.

> **Reading my graphs.** Throughout the book, I will talk about several graphics like this one. Those of you who took economics in college have seen more than your fair share of these graphs. For those of you who did not, let me explain how to read them. The X axis, or the numbers along the bottom, represents the amount of sales volume in a distributor's organization. It is zero at the far left and increases as it moves to the right. The Y axis shows the amount of distributor earnings; these are on the left side. It, too, begins at zero at the bottom and increases as it moves up. So if a line is flat, it means that sales volume is increasing, but earnings are staying the same. If it's going up, that means that as sales volume increases, earnings are also increasing. The steeper the line, the faster earnings are increasing. If the line is going down, then as sales volume increases, earnings decrease.

As you can see from the graph in Figure 7, a company can control the angle of the earnings line by the percentage paid on sales volume. If the percentage is higher, the earnings of the distributors will grow more quickly. However, the steeper the line and the faster the earnings growth, the sooner the line flattens out as sales volume moves out of the distributor's payline. The first line would have ten percent down three levels and the second line would have five percent down six levels. They both have thirty percent payout, but the second goes deeper into the downline. The earnings grow more slowly, but for a longer period of time. The reason the line flattens out is that sales volume moves out of the distributor's payline more quickly in the ten percent example.

Figure 7

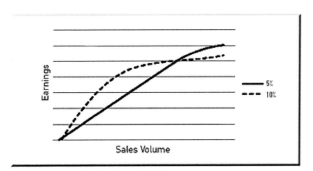

Sometimes these percentages are paid on *personal* volume. In that case, they're typically called *unilevel* commissions. In other cases, the percentages are paid on *group* volume. In those cases, they're typically called *generation* or *leader* commissions. Let's look at each of these sub-types.

Unilevel Commissions. In a unilevel plan, distributors receive defined percentages on the *personal* volume of their downlines. The requirements that distributors must meet to receive these commissions are usually relatively minimal.

This easy requirement is one of the advantages of this type of commission. Once a sponsor signs up a distributor, as long as the sponsor stays active, he or she receives commissions on any product the distributor sells. People like this plan because it's so easy. The weakness of the plan is that distributors may have the perception that they don't have to continue to build their organizations in order to receive commissions—therefore, what incentive do they have to continue to work? One way companies encourage distributors to continue to build their organizations is by adding additional ranks that require a distributor to build an organization in order to receive the benefit of getting paid deeper. Figure 8 shows an example of this kind of plan.

Understanding Multi-Level Commissions

Figure 8

Pure Unilevel	Modified Unilevel Bonus Plan			
Pure Unilevel	1 Star	2 Star	3 Star	4 Star
5%	5%	5%	5%	5%
5%	5%	5%	5%	5%
5%	5%	5%	5%	5%
5%		5%	5%	5%
5%			5%	5%
5%				5%

Generation or Leader Commissions. This is the second type of level commission. A graph of a generation commission looks virtually identical to the one we used earlier to illustrate a level commission.

The big difference, however, between a generation commission and a unilevel commission is that generation commissions pay distributors on group volume rather than on the personal volume of their downline. This means that salespeople, sales leaders, and dreambuilders can all qualify to receive a generation commission if they qualify. These commissions have more difficult qualifications, usually including a personal sales volume requirement and a group sales volume requirement. Generation commissions are designed to *pull up into a distributor's payline* the people who are doing big business. With a well-designed generation commission, distributors receive payouts on a certain number of levels of *hubs of activity;* each level of activity is typically called a "generation."

Companies create a hub of activity in two ways. First, they create fairly challenging requirements for a distributor to become a leader and to continue to be paid as a leader. Second, most companies use compression to reach down and pay distributors on these hubs of activity.

A company can use this type of commission to pay the sales management. It's the commission type that allows distributors to be well compensated after they've built large organizations. Historically, dream-builders who earn the "big bucks" earn the vast majority of that money with a generation commission.

Pros and Cons: The major strengths of the level commission are:

The level commission is the easiest commission type to understand. Over the years it has been used by hundreds of companies, employing many iterations, and its behaviors are well known.

It can be designed to create the stable earnings base, which is critical for a successful commission plan. Once this stable earnings base is in place, then other commission types can be used to target other important aspects of a commission plan.

It's a *non-blocking* commission, which means that a distributor is always paid on the first several levels of his or her distributors' organizations. It isn't blocked when someone in the sponsoring distributor's downline reaches the same rank. See the discussion of differential commissions for more on blocking.

A couple of challenges are inherent with level commissions

There is typically no specific incentive for a distributor to go out and do the next $100 worth of volume today, because his earnings are going to grow at a steady rate no matter when he builds sales volume; whereas, some other commissions can be designed to create a sense of urgency for increasing group volume. No sense of urgency is built in to the level commission

With level commissions you often see *stacking*. (In just a second, I'll talk about stacking.)

Another problem results from the gaps in the payout caused by inactivity. For example, if a distributor receives five percent down three levels, and distributors on two of those levels are no longer active, then the distributor gets frustrated and wants the company to terminate the two inactive levels to allow active distributors who are deeper in the organization to move up to a level where the distributor can get paid on them. This puts companies in a tough spot. Should they terminate inactive distributors quickly to maximize commissions, or should they work to reactivate distributors for the long-term good of the company? Up until about 1985, these were the only two choices. Modern level commissions can compensate for the problem of inactivity by using a system called *compression*. (I talk about compression in detail at the end of this section)

Related Issue

Stacking. Now we come to the problem of *stacking,* the bane of level commissions. The concept is easy. For example, a distributor realizes that instead of receiving five percent on the sales of his first level, he can receive ten percent by sponsoring his wife as his first level and placing the rest of his organization under her. Then he realizes that he could make fifteen percent by sponsoring his mother under his wife, and so on. A second method is for four friends to get together and sponsor person B under person A, C under B, and D under C. Then all four of them sponsor all of their prospects under person D, splitting the three-level commissions.

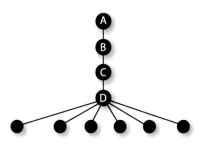

What's wrong with that? The reason a company sets up a level commission is to reward the upline for building the organization. Stacking defeats this objective. If everyone stacked, no one would receive any downline commissions! If stacking becomes rampant, the net effect is the same as simply paying a one-level commission with no downline commissions.

It's interesting to talk to people who stack and point out to them that if their downline stacks, then they won't make any money. Almost universally, they'll tell you that they don't allow people in their downlines to stack! If a company wants to have a level commission and have it work the way it's designed, the company must find a way to eliminate stacking.

There are three ways for companies to deal with stacking:

1. The most successful method is to *make it unprofitable* by creating rules that make it unprofitable. (I discuss rules in detail in Chapter Five.) For example, you can make a rule that specifies that in order to receive commissions, distributors must have $1,000 of volume in the downline and no more than half of that amount can come from any one downline leg. Now, in order to stack four people, the distributor has to put a second leg under each of them that generates $500 of volume. It's possible, but expensive.

2. The second method is *enforcement*. The company watches to see if anyone is stacking and punishes those who are. (Trust me—the upline will inform the company if someone is stacking.) The problem with this method is that a company never wants to put itself in the position of having to punish its distributors; it's bad for relations. Besides, sometimes it's perfectly legitimate for a distributor to sponsor his wife, but the anti-stacking police can't always determine whether what has happened is stacking or legitimate business.

3. *Ask distributors not to stack.* I've never seen it work, but several times when I've told companies that their commission plans are susceptible to stacking, they don't want to follow either of the procedures above, so they just make this request.

> **Three responses to stacking:**
>
> passive—set up rules so that stacking doesn't work
> active—penalize the distributors who stack their organizations
> head-in-the-sand—assume the distributors won't stack

Compression. *Compression* is probably the greatest innovation to come along in the world of level commissions. Around since about 1985, it has become so prevalent that it's rare to see a level commission that doesn't include compression.

Compression is a technique that keeps inactive or non-qualified distributors from occupying a payout level in a level commission plan. For example, if I sponsor Fred and he doesn't qualify to earn a level commission, I receive commissions on his first-level distributors as though I'd personally sponsored them.

Figure 9

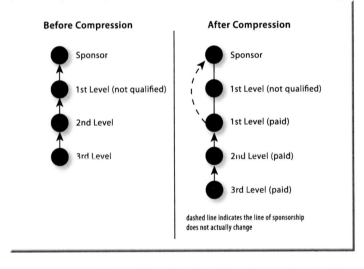

Furthermore, if one of these first-level distributors isn't qualified, that person's first-level distributors are also treated as my first level. This goes on until a qualified distributor appears in the organization to occupy the first level. Then the process is repeated until we find a qualified distributor to occupy the second level, and so forth.

Compression solves a couple of problems. It puts more money into the hands of the distributors, and it encourages distributors to work with their downlines, even those many levels of sponsorship down the genealogy.

Another benefit is that distributors are paid around their inactive or non-qualifying downline distributors, but compression leaves these inactive distributors in place and gives them time to build their organizations. This approach doesn't hurt the upline. Before compression, it was common for companies to take away a distributor's rank or terminate the distributorship entirely if he or she was inactive for even a month or two. Obviously, this approach was discouraging to distributors struggling to build an organization. Now, most companies allow distributors several non-qualifying months without taking away their rank or terminating them. The company doesn't pay them for this rank, but it doesn't embarrass them by taking away the rank. Companies with this type of system refer to *pin rank*, the rank the distributor has achieved, and *paid rank*, the rank at which the distributor is qualified to be paid for the current month.

The last problem compression solves is the problem of *breakage*. Let me explain that concept. If a company doesn't compress out non-qualified distributors, the unqualified distributors accumulate commissions. But since they don't qualify, the company keeps the commission money. Breakage is the difference between what a company's commission plan *can pay* and what it actually *does pay*. Most plans have some breakage, but the problem with allowing this particular type of breakage is that if a company is having a period of declining sales, then this type of breakage increases as a percentage of sales. When this happens, distributor checks go down even faster than sales do, and that is something no company wants.

This is the point where I usually point out the disadvantages of a feature, but I can't think of any disadvantages of compression.

Dynamic compression is an interesting variation on compression. Standard compression, as I mentioned, typically still doesn't pay out all of the commission money. Remember the chart showing payout on a typical level commission plan? Dynamic compression comes into play only for a distributor who qualifies as a 1-Star and has fourth- and fifth-level distributors. One challenge of dynamic compression is that the term "dynamic compression" can have several meanings. Every time I use it, people think of different things. It's not well understood.

In one company that implemented dynamic compression, the company executives thought it meant one thing, the field thought another thing, and the programmers thought another thing. It was in effect for over a year before the company executives realized that the programmers hadn't programmed it as they understood it, and the brochure described something entirely different. So one problem with dynamic compression is that the way I describe it in this book doesn't match what a lot of people think. However, *this is how I understand it*. Simply stated, dynamic compression pays out all levels of a level commission. So in our example, it would attempt to always pay commission on levels four and five.

The rules of standard compression say that a distributor is compressed out if the distributor is inactive or non-qualified. A distributor who is active and qualified, but doesn't qualify for fourth- or fifth-level commissions, won't receive the commission for those levels; it becomes breakage. Is this good or bad? Once again, the answer depends on what you're trying to accomplish. Dynamic compression compresses out not only those who are inactive or non-qualified; it also compresses out people who don't qualify for a specific level of commission. In this case, it would compress out the unqualified distributors on those levels they don't qualify for, and pay the fourth- and fifth-level commissions to their upline.

The advantage of dynamic compression is that it lets a company pay a leader even deeper into the downline. The disadvantage of dynamic compression is that if it's difficult to qualify for a level, then distributors may be paid down many levels because few people in their downline are qualified. The result is that a company pays out a lot of money. Another problem occurs when one day someone on such a distributor's first level does qualify. All of that income then moves to the distributor's first level, causing a sudden and drastic downturn in earnings for that person.

Rather than using dynamic compression, a company may try other ways to use the breakage to motivate desired behavior. It's possible, for example, to take the income the company doesn't pay out on the unpaid levels and put it into pools and other incentives. However, having said that, I must point out that many distributors like the fact that there are no unpaid levels.

Just remember that dynamic compression is not the only way to ensure full payout, and full payout is not necessarily the correct approach.

On the Soapbox

Is Full Payout Fairer?

One argument for dynamic compression is to make the plan pay out its maximum so there's no breakage back to the company. This is a good time to have the discussion about whether breakage is always a bad thing? There are four reasons why not paying the theoretical maximum payout can be a reasonable approach for a company.

1. When the company is smaller, the payout is less. Over time, as the company's sales volume increases into the millions of dollars per month, the payout increases. In a sense, this is fairer to the distributor force, because as the company gets bigger, it should achieve operational efficiencies and should be able to afford higher payouts. As the company can afford more, it pays more.

2. It's a myth that a company must pay out its maximum. In order for a company to be fair, it should pay out what it budgeted to pay out. Now, a company with a plan that has a theoretical maximum payout of fifty percent may have only budgeted forty-three percent because it knows it will never pay the maximum. Some types of commission plans are not designed to pay out the maximum.

3. Perception is reality. A commission plan that theoretically could pay out seventy percent and only pays out forty percent gives that company a competitive advantage over a company with a plan that could pay out fifty percent and actually does pay out fifty percent. This is true because the market is going to perceive that the

On the Soapbox

Continued

seventy-percent plan pays more than the fifty-percent plan, even though the fifty-percent plan is actually paying more. I don't know if that perception is fair, but why do companies price things at 99¢ (Jason – fix this cents sign to look good) instead of $1.00? Because it doesn't seem as much—it's a matter of perception.

4. If a company has a plan that could pay a maximum of fifty percent but usually pays only forty percent, in certain cases it will pay fifty percent. This happens when someone performs the specific activities the plan is designed to reward. The plan is paying distributors that extra ten percent because they're doing what the company wants them to do, and that's better for both the distributors and the company. If the distributors do exactly what the company wants them to do, then the company is growing successfully and can afford the higher payout. If they're not doing what the company wants them to do, then the payout goes down. Then the company can afford to run marketing campaigns or whatever it must do to get sales moving upwards again.

In my experience, full payout is not a hard-and-fast rule.

Rollup. *Rollup,* as I define it, isn't used much any more, but all of these techniques come back around, so I'll mention it here. Rollup is a technique used instead of compression to create full payout. Under this method, rather than keeping the breakage created by unqualified distributors, the commission program calculates what unqualified distributors would earn if they were qualified. Then, instead of paying *them,* the commissions are paid to the first upline qualified distributor, or, in the language of the industry, we "roll up" the commissions to the first qualified distributor.

There is confusion between compression and rollup, and many people say rollup when they're actually thinking about what I call compression.

Why isn't rollup used much any more? This system rewards a sponsor who has unqualified distributors on his or her first level. Furthermore, the upline has no incentive to encourage unqualified distributors in the downline to qualify. If a sponsor's downline starts to qualify, he or she no longer receives those rolled-up commissions; instead, the sponsor receives only a percentage of the sales volume. Since that change always means a drastically reduced income for the sponsor, he or she is unlikely to encourage it. In short, rollup seems to be a bad way of ensuring a full payout.

Another problem is that rollup effectively rewards stacking. As we said before, the most effective anti-stacking mechanism is to make it difficult enough to qualify for commissions that people are discouraged from stacking. But with rollup, even if the stacked distributors don't qualify, the distributor who did the stacking gets the rolled-up commissions anyway. Some disincentive!

Summary: Level commissions have been the mainstay of commission plans for the last twenty-five years and all indications are that they will remain so for the foreseeable future. They provide the backbone of stability that any commission plan needs to be successful.

Differential commissions

Overview: The differential commission is a tool to target earnings. This graph shows the difference in earnings, to an individual distributor, between a unilevel commission and a differential commission. Both commissions have an overall payout of twenty percent. You will notice that, in this example, at first the payout on the differential commission is less than that on the unilevel. Then the differential quickly grows to around $500 a month.

Figure 10

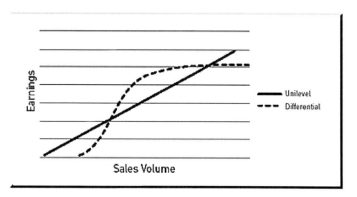

This kind of commission targets a specific activity. In this example, it targets salespeople to get them quickly to the $500-a-month mark. Other plans may target building group volume or building downline activity. As you can see, the major benefit of a differential commission is that it allows the company to target a specific activity and rewards the distributors who do it. The earnings accumulate to the distributors who are doing those specific things rewarded by the commission. Whereas a level commission is designed to spread the wealth, a differential commission is designed to maximize commissions to those who are doing what the plan is designed to reward.

The two names typically used to describe differential commissions within commission plans are *stairstep* and *overlapping infinity* commissions.

Usage: Because the differential commission can reward specific activities and tends to target earnings to specific distributors, it has been successfully used as a salesperson commission.

However, these same characteristics tend to make it generally unsuitable for sales management commissions where it's important to spread earnings between several sales leaders and dream-builders. Some companies have used an overlapping infinity commission, which is a differential commission, as part of the sales management commission package and have had success as long as it's only a *part* of the overall commission package.

The Details: The concept of a differential commission plan seems simple, but it's difficult to explain. A company decides on the total percentage it wants to pay—for example, twenty percent— and then decides what percentage each rank should receive.

For our example, let's say that a 1-Star receives five percent, a 2-Star receives ten percent, a 3-Star receives fifteen percent, and a 4-Star receives twenty percent. Starting with the person who sold the product and moving up through that person's upline, the seller is paid his or her percentage. If that distributor doesn't receive the full percentage because he or she isn't at the highest rank, then the payout moves up to that person's sponsor.

This commission pays the difference between the percentage the distributor qualifies for and the percentage the sponsor qualifies for. This is where the term "differential commission" comes from. Therefore, if the sponsor is at the same or a lower rank as the downline person, the sponsor doesn't receive anything on that transaction. If at a higher rank, that person receives the percentage he or she is eligible for, less what has already been paid to the downline on that transaction. (In other words, a person gets the difference between what he or she qualifies for and what has already been paid). The calculation keeps going upline until the total percentage assigned to this commission type is paid; in this example, twenty percent will be paid out. This commission type always pays the full percentage assigned to this commission, and never more, and typically never less.

Figure 11

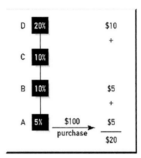

Remember, Appendix D contains some sample exercises to help you work through and understand differential commissions. If you've never worked with a differential commission, working through these exercises should clarify for you the way this commission pays.

Stairstep form of differential. For many years, the most popular form of this commission type has been the *stairstep* commission. Stairstep is the commission plan that's designed to pay the salespeople for the time they must spend to take care of their consumers. Stairstep plans typically pay between zero and twenty-five percent. Below is an example of how a stairstep plan is charted.

Figure 12

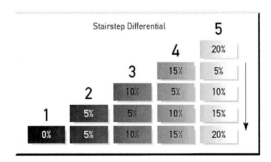

When distributors join a company, they are on the lowest "step." As they meet the requirements to climb the steps, they earn increasing percentages on their personal and group volume.

Section Two: The Building Blocks

Remember, Appendix D contains some sample exercises to help you work through and understand differential commissions. If you've never worked with a differential commission, working through these exercises should clarify for you the way this commission pays.

Stepped infinity form of the differential. The second major variation of the differential commission is the *stepped infinity* commission. The stepped infinity takes its name because it's possible for distributors to be paid on their entire organization. However, it's important to realize that someone in the downline who is eligible for the same percentage of this commission does block that portion of the commission from that point on down. So it's important to understand that in this context "infinity" means you *might* earn all the way to the bottom of your organization (in other words, "to infinity"), but that you also may be blocked by someone in your downline.

A sample stepped infinity pays in this manner:

Figure 13

```
$500,000 of organization volume  - 2 percent
$1,000,000 of organization volume - 4 percent
$2,000,000 of organization volume - 6 percent
```

So if I have $2,000,000 of organization volume, do I make six percent on all of it? Maybe, if there's no one under me with at least $500,000.

So what's the difference between stairstep and stepped infinity? Nothing, really, except how much downline volume it takes to qualify and the percentage paid for each. Stairstep is for people just getting into the business and is an excellent way of compensating salespeople for keeping their consumers happy. It's the core commission for the product evangelists and the salespeople who are just starting out.

Stepped infinity, on the other hand, is at the opposite end of the spectrum. It's only paid to the highest of the high dream-builders.

Companies often use it as the motivator for top dream-builders to continue working after they've reached the top of the commission plan.

On the Soapbox

The INFINITY myth

I've never seen a true infinity commission. If you have a commission that pays down infinite levels on your organization, and pays on infinite volume—in other words, on all the volume your organization generates—then the company's payout can be infinite! Those are the facts, and the laws of mathematics seem to ensure that no one will ever find a way around them.

There are two kinds of commissions that some contend can break this law of math. The first is actually called the infinity commission. This commission typically pays top leaders one to six percent on their organizations. The method companies use to try to make them infinite is to set the qualifications so high that only a few can qualify for it. The thinking is that it's infinite because it will be a long time before someone in the organization qualifies for it and blocks the sponsor from getting commissions from that downline.

The second type of infinity commission is binary. But as I point out in the section on binary in Chapter Nine, a distributor is paid on unlimited levels (infinity), but can only be paid on a certain amount of sales volume.

Pros and Cons: The differential commission has several strong points:

It's a good way of making sure that the salesperson gets enough commission to continue to work with consumers and new distributors.

It's self-adjusting in that, if consumers and new distributors become more involved, the commissions automatically start to migrate to them. This allows the cream to rise to the top. The distributors are in charge of their own destinies. They know in advance what's required, and they always get the reward if they perform the predefined tasks. This plan also rewards those who build an organization that has a good balance between width and depth. It does so by making sure that if they have the width, they will always be in a percentage higher than the individual downline organizations.

Differential commissions are not susceptible to stacking, meaning that even if an organization stacks, it usually doesn't take commissions away from the upline.

The weakness of differential commissions are:

You cannot build an entire commission plan around a differential commission. Companies need other commission types to build a stable earnings base.

It's the most difficult to understand of all the commission types. Even though it's been in use for many years by some of the most successful companies, very few people can accurately calculate a differential commission.

Differential commissions are a blocking commission. In many cases, at some point, both you and your first levels are at the same commission percentage. When this occurs, you're "blocked" from commissions. You don't make anything on that leg of your downline. Once you and your first level both reach the top percentage of the differential commission, the blocking becomes permanent. Blocking is the reason that differential commissions need to be combined with other commission types to create balanced commission plans.

Related Issues

Promotion methods. There are several variations for promotion in a plan that uses differential commissions. As distributors advance to higher ranks, they earn a higher percentage. A company has to decide exactly when to make the rank advancement effective. There are three methods:

1. *Break on the Fly.* The distributor moves to the new percentage as soon as the qualifications are met, right in the middle of an order if necessary.

2. *Qualify/Effective Month.* The distributor is paid the full month at whatever percentage he or she started with, even if he or she advances mid-month.

3. *Retroactive.* The distributor is paid the full month at the *new* rank percentage, even if he or she advances mid-month.

4. *Start Over.* The distributor has to start over at the lowest rank every month until a distributor reaches a certain rank, and then the company switches to one of the other methods.

Each of these variations has its own advantages. That discussion is beyond the scope of this book, but a company does need to consider them when defining a commission plan.

Summary: The differential has proven to be a valuable component for a long-term stable and successful network marketing business. It falls in and out of favor as the years pass, but has weathered the test of time and has proven to be a winner.

Single-level commissions

Overview: I walked around and argued with myself for a long time as to whether this is actually a type of differential commission or its own type. I argued both the pros and cons with my wife, and she remained silent. Finally, she told me that if I ever brought it up again, I would be sorry for a very long time! Actually, she never said that. After eighteen years of being married to me, she's learned how to ignore me when she needs to.

I decided that single-level rated its own type because the behavior is significantly different from that of differential commissions, and it's clearly not a multi-level commission. So, what is a single-level commission, and what is it used for?

Single-level commissions pay the entire commission to one distributor. Typically, the commission is paid on group volume, and the percentage of the single-level commission varies depending on factors such as the distributor's rank and group volume.

Single-level commissions are often called "qualified sales leader" commissions.

Usage: Single-level commissions are often used as salesperson commissions, because the commission is paid to one person, and is often a variable percentage. It's easy to target this commission to a distributor who meets very specific qualifications. This is the most targeted of all commissions; it pays one distributor and one distributor only.

This means that it's almost wholly unsuited to paying sales leaders, and is seldom used for anything except paying a distributor on their group volume.

The Details: Single-level commissions are similar to differential commissions in that they're typically put in place to reward specific activities. However, there are several differences:

1. On or Off: Since only one person earns the entire commission, it's like an on/off switch. The distributor works hard to qualify, but until he does, he doesn't make any money. Once the distributor does qualify, he makes the entire commission amount. If someone in his downline qualifies, that person takes away the entire commission on that leg all at once. Now the first distributor is earning nothing again. In contrast, a differential commission is more like a volume control knob. As a distributor starts to qualify, she starts to earn part of the commission, and slowly takes part of the commission from her upline. When someone in her downline starts to qualify, it slowly takes the commission from her and pays it to that downline distributor.

Understanding Multi-Level Commissions

Figure 14

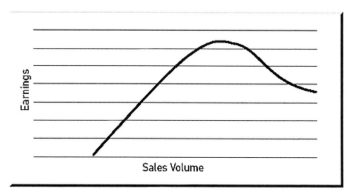

2. Variable Earnings: This type of commission often has a range of percentages that the distributor can earn, based on some qualification. For example, a 3-Star may earn between ten and fifteen percent, depending on his or her group volume for a given month. Whatever percentage is not paid out is typically retained by the company.

Pros and Cons: The benefits of a single-level commission are:

The variable commission percentage gives companies an easy way to create an extra reward for its top salespeople by paying them a higher commission percentage on their group volume without significantly raising the company's overall commission payout.

The single-level commission used in conjunction with a level commission has some of the characteristics of the differential commission; however, it's easier to understand. That can be an advantage in some situations.

The company can create very specific rewards for very specific group volume activity.

The disadvantages of a single-level payout are:

All commissions go to a single distributor. If a company also wants to reward a product evangelist, it must create another commission type, such as the level commission. It can hurt morale when a distributor is at the top percent of the variable percent payout and someone in the downline breaks away. The breakaway distributor not only reduces the sales volume the distributor is paid on, but also the percentage earned on the remaining sales volume as well.

It's the least able of all the commission types to stand on its own, so companies that use single-level commissions typically combine it with at least two other commission types.

Summary

Over the years, I've seen quite a few plans that included this type of commission. Companies wishing to build a nice reward for achieving a certain rank included a single-level commission that paid on the distributor's entire downline down to the next person of that rank. You can see that a commission attached to a high rank could end up as a pretty substantial portion of a distributor's check. When properly designed, a single-level commission can be a very effective part of a commission plan.

Pool commissions

Overview: A pool commission is excellent for targeting a very, very specific behavior. Here is an example of a pool commission:

A company has a million dollars in sales volume and it sets up a "one percent, equal shares pool commission" that targets 3-Stars who generate $2,000 in personal sales volume. One percent of sales volume is $10,000, thus establishing the size of the pool. Now, in our example, we will assume that fifty people qualify for the pool. Dividing $10,000 by fifty means checks of $200 per person. You can see that this makes an immediate impact because it raises a person's earnings by ten percent of his or her personal volume.

The advantages of a pool commission are that it's immediate and that it targets a very specific behavior. If a company is trying to encourage a certain behavior in its distributors, a pool commission can really make a difference. The flip side is that if the company becomes wildly successful and the qualifications have not been well designed, suddenly five hundred people qualify for the pool, and it's now worth only $20. It no longer has value. Pool commissions, then, can be a double-edged sword because the pool can devalue quickly. Yet they can be good for short-term or for targeted incentives as long as the incentive is high. Pool commissions are the most flexible of all commissions

Usage: Because of that flexibility, companies can use pool commissions to enhance both sales commissions and sales management commissions, although it's almost never the primary commission in either case. Why, then, do companies use pools? The answer is quite simple. Look at our previous example. Suppose the company wants to increase by $200 the earnings of its 3-Stars who generate $2,000 per month of group volume, but want to make sure that it doesn't cost the company more than one percent. Of course, a company's decision-makers can check the numbers and look at history, but when they put a new commission in place, they never know how many more people will qualify, so instead they use a pool commission. A pool commission is a good way to keep the commission payout in line, but create some innovative commissions.

The Details: A pool commission has two parts. One is the amount of the pool. The company usually designates some percentage of sales. Most pools are a couple of percent of sales or less. The other part is determining the qualification rules for participating in the pool: for example, anyone who achieves $500 in personal sales in a given month, or anyone who has $1,000,000 of downline sales volume.

Companies typically use pool commissions for one of three reasons.

1. To give an added incentive to reach an intermediate rank in the commission plan. For example, if a company wants to encourage distributors to achieve the rank of 3-Star and to earn at least $400 per month, a pool commission is designed to pay $100 to all qualified 3-Stars helps to ensure that the earnings goals are met and gives an added incentive to achieve the rank.

2. To add additional earning capabilities to a plan in which dream-builders will hit an earnings ceiling. For example, a company might divide one percent of sales among all the 9-Star distributors in a proportional-shares pool based on each 9-Star's organizational sales volume. This pool can encourage the dream-builders to continue to build their organization even though most of their downline growth may be beyond their payline.

3. To fund incentives like car programs and other targeted or special purpose incentives.

There are two major variations of pools. In the *equal-shares pool*, everyone who qualifies gets an equal share of the pool. In the *proportional-shares pool*, everyone who qualifies earns the same proportion that their downline contributed to the overall contribution to the pool.

As an example of these two types, let's say that anyone who does at least $500 in personal sales in a given month qualifies for a one percent pool. Now that you know who can qualify for the pool and how much the payout is, the only thing left to decide is how to divide the money. If it's a *proportional-shares pool* according to how much qualifying volume a distributor had in relation to the others in the pool, a distributor with $500 in qualifying volume would receive half as much as a distributor with $1,000 in qualifying volume. If it's an *equal-shares pool*, if 100 people qualify and there was $10,000 in the pool, then each would get $100.

Which is best? That depends on what a company is trying to accomplish. If they're trying to motivate people to reach new heights, the proportional-shares formula is the best. But if, for example, the company wants to ensure that all qualified 3-Star distributors make at least $400 per month, then the equal-shares pool is the best.

The strength of a pool commission lies in its versatility and in its ability to target a specific group. In other words, a company can create a pool commission to target any group in the company. If a company wants to encourage recruiting, it can define a proportional-shares pool that includes anyone who sponsors more than three new people who have $100 in sales volume. Or if the company is worried that its top distributors are capping out in their earnings too fast, it can set up a pool based on organizational volume in which only distributors with more than $1,000,000 in downline sales can participate.

Pros and Cons: Let's review some of the pros of a pool commission:

It's an excellent way of rewarding very specific activities with very limited payout.

It can fill in some of the "flat spots" in a commission plan.

A pool is a good way of encouraging distributors to continue to build even after reaching the top rank.

What are some of the disadvantages of a pool commission?

If the pool isn't properly designed, shares of the pool can devalue as the company grows.

Pools can be so targeted that companies have to make sure that they're targeting the right activities.

Summary

It seems that every company that uses pool commissions either loves them or hates them. No one seems to be in the middle. This is an indication of the importance of "doing them right." The other important issue to remember about the pool commission is not to center too much of a company's commissions around pools. Use them only as finishing-touch commissions.

Conclusion

In this chapter, I've laid the basic building blocks of the many hundreds of variations, mutations, iterations, and mutilations of commission plans. I've seen all of them built using these few commission types as building blocks.

Each commission type accomplishes a specific goal. When used in combination, these commission types can serve to reward the specific activities a company is trying to encourage. Here is a brief summary of the specific payout characteristics of each commission type:

1. **Level commission**: Always spreads the earnings among several distributors. This commission type spreads earnings out more than any other commission type. However, it doesn't target earnings to specific distributor types. Level commissions are the backbone of sales management commissions.

2. **Differential Commission:** Targets and accumulates earnings to distributors who accomplish specific goals as defined by the commission type. The great thing about a well-designed differential commission is that it can be designed to put commissions in the hands of the salesperson, or split commissions between the salesperson and the product evangelist.

> **On the Soapbox**
>
> It often seems that there are "new types" of commission being invented. Binary, matching, coding commissions, Australian 2-up, in their time, have all been promoted as new and revolutionary commissions. But all of them are still variations on the four types of commissions.

3. **Single-level commission**: Pays earnings to distributors who achieve specific ranks or downline volumes. It's an extremely targeted commission that's paid on downline volume.

4. **Pool commission**: Rewards rank achievement or other very specific activities and is not paid on downline sales. Here again, this is an extremely targeted commission that is *not* paid on downline volume. If a company is trying to create a specific reward to distributors for achieving specific criteria, this is a great way of doing it.

In Chapter Nine, we'll see how all these commission types work when they're put together in a real-life commission plan.

Understanding Multi-Level Commissions

Chapter Five

Key Topics

The four kinds of rules 93
Rank advancement rules 95
Reversion 101
Monthly qualification rules 104
Other rules to consider 106
Summary 107

Understanding Multi-Level Commissions

What are the *rules* that govern commission plans?

Rules are what give the character to a compensation plan. They make it bitter as vinegar or sweet as sugar. If a company becomes known for front-end loading, it's because the rules encouraged and allowed or required it, *not* because the company chose one type of commission plan or another. So if you want to know why distributors of a certain company consistently act a certain way, you will almost always find your answer in their rules.

Commissions define what a distributor will be paid. Rules define what a distributor must do in order to be paid. A company makes two types of rules: the positive motivational rules that create incentive for distributors to continually grow their businesses, sometimes referred to as "the carrot," and the negative rules that define what the company will do to them if they get out of line, also known as "the stick." Companies should try to have as many "carrots" as possible and as few "sticks" as necessary.

> *Commissions define what a distributor will be paid. Rules define what a distributor must do in order to be paid.*

The four kinds of rules

Basically, there are four kinds of rules:

1. Rules that govern distributor advancement from rank to rank.
2. Rules that define the qualifications a distributor must meet in order to receive the various commissions.
3. Rules to ensure that distributors don't create legal or ethical problems for the company.*
4. Rules to ensure that distributors maintain ethical behavior while building their organizations.*

Rules are, of course, a way of life, but every rule a company sets creates a potential conflict with its distributors. *A company must think*

---
* I will leave these issues to your attorney.

Understanding Multi-Level Commissions

them through carefully. I often see rules in companies' policies and procedures that were copied from another company, even though the reason for the rule doesn't apply to this company or is long gone. It also surprises me that even when a company is made aware of this, many will decide to leave the rule "just in case."

The *rules* of a plan affect payout to distributors just as surely as the definitions of the commissions themselves. Furthermore, the rules often have almost as much *effect* on the company's overall payout as the commissions percentages themselves do.

The rules designate the qualifications a distributor must meet in order to move up in rank, achieve a higher percentage on the group volume of his or her organization, receive a sales commission, or whatever benefits that distributor is trying to attain.

Each company sets up rules according to its own needs. However, a company's commission plan will almost certainly have to include two categories of rules: *commissions qualification* rules and *rank advancement* rules. Distributors want to be able to depend on a clearly defined set of rules that tell them what they have to do to be paid each month and what they have to do to advance in rank. Since these rules govern the way distributors build their businesses, the rules need to make sense, be fair, and most of all, be consistent.

It's important that the company not change the basic framework of rank advancement rules once they're in place. This is important, since distributors will build their businesses based on the rules a company has in place. For the company to change the rules is to destroy the value of the organization that a distributor has spent months or even years building. I think the day will come when top distributors won't build a downline unless they have some contractual assurances that a company won't continually change the rules that define the basic structure of the commission plan. Obviously, companies need the ability to make changes to deal with the economic realities of a changing marketplace, but under normal conditions there's no reason for the company to change the basic structure of the commission plan.

Basically, then, a company builds its qualification rules to set the distributors on the path the company wants them to follow, and then puts in a system of commissions that rewards them for following that path.

There are two kinds of qualification rules: those to qualify for rank advancement, and those to qualify to receive commissions each month. This is where the issue of having lots of ranks and lots of commission types creates a challenge for a company. The more ranks a company has, the more rules are required to advance from rank to rank and to qualify to earn each of those commissions. In addition, the commission plan description becomes more complex. The more complex the commission plan becomes, the harder it is to explain, the more time you need to explain it, the more confused people are, the more consumer service people the company has to employ—you see the problem.

Companies can help alleviate this situation by having a consistent method of advancing from rank to rank. The advancement rules must set up a logical, consistent system for commission payout for each rank, for achieving a rank in the first place, and for maintaining qualifications. In general, a company should make the rules as simple as is feasible to achieve the desired results.

Rank advancement rules

In most companies, the distributors advance in rank by building their organizations and increasing their downline sales volume. The best way to start creating the rules is to think about the various types of distributors and what they need to do as they grow their businesses. A company always needs to keep *the top rank* in mind as it defines the rules for the other ranks.

Another thing to remember is that once distributors reach the highest rank, it's tempting for them to quit building their organization. When a company defines the top rank, it needs to make sure that when people do achieve that rank, their earnings are in line with the respect the company wants the rank to command. For example, if a "4-Star Diamond" rank is the top rank, and some distributors at that rank are earning only $2,000 a month, it won't command much respect. This is especially problematic if some 4-Star Diamonds are earning $2,000 and some are earning $100,000.

With these ideas in mind, let's talk about the specific rules companies use for rank advancement and commission qualifications. The ten most common qualifications are:

1. *Personal sales volume:* In most companies, a distributor must have a certain amount of personal sales each month. Before defining this requirement, a company must take its product line into account; the requirement should be based on the number of people it would take to consume that much product each month. Sometimes, as a distributor becomes a sales leader, this requirement rises. However, as they achieve the highest ranks, this requirement does not normally continue to rise; often, it drops back to the initial requirement.

2. *Group volume:* The first big question is, "What is my group?" Companies that use group volume as a qualification have a rank in their commission plan that is defined as a group or leader rank. It's also often called a "breakaway" rank because it's earned when the distributor breaks away from his sponsor's group. In most companies, a distributor's group volume includes anyone for whom he is the first upline distributor who has not achieved this group rank.

3. *Level volume:* This is the amount of sales volume within a certain number of levels in a distributor's downline organization. There are several variations of this qualification. For example, sometimes compression is used.

4. *Organization volume*: This is the volume a distributor's entire downline develops. It can be a very useful method of qualifying distributors for the higher ranks of a plan. One common addition to this qualification is not to allow more than a certain percentage of the qualification to come from any one leg of a distributor's organization: for example, one million dollars of sales volume with no more that $300,000 from any one leg.

5. *Downline rank achievements*: A company can require that in order to be a 2-Star, distributors must have three 1-Stars somewhere in their organization.

6. *Number of downline legs of a certain rank*: For example, require three separate downline legs, with at least one 3-Star somewhere in each downline leg.

7. *Number of first level distributors*: There are four ways that a company counts first level distributors for purposes of qualification.

    a. The number of actual first level distributors.

    b. The number of qualified first level distributors.

    c. The number of qualified first level distributors, but apply compression as first level distributors are counted.

    d. The number of qualified distributors of a specific rank or higher. For example, to qualify for to become a 4-Star, a company may require a distributor to have five first level distributors of rank 3-star or above.

8. *Personal sponsored/sales volume:* This is the amount of sales volume of the personally sponsored distributors or consumers.

9. *Monthly Autoship volume:* Many companies are now promoting Monthly Autoship programs, and so, part of their qualifications is the amount of sales volume generated by the autoship orders of personally sponsored/enrolled distributors of a distributor. These are orders that once placed, are automatically shipped to the consumer each month. Companies typically create this qualification in conjunction with a reduction of a personal volume requirement or a group volume requirement. In other words, a distributor can do the regular qualification OR do the reduced qualification along with the autoship qualification.

10. *Trained and certified:* This requirement can be very valuable in ensuring a knowledgeable sales force. However, it's the least used of all the requirements.

Once a company decides what qualifications to use, it's important to build consistency as a distributor moves from rank to rank. A distributor shouldn't have to build one way to become a sales leader and then change methods to get to the next rank. A company shouldn't, for example, have the rules for all ranks encourage distributors to build their downline deep, and then switch to having them build their downline wide in order to advance to the top rank.

In most cases, a distributor needs to sponsor a number of people in order to find a few good leaders. One of the great debates that has raged in the industry for years is how wide an organization a distributor should build while building deep. This debate is more than academic. When companies design their plans, they create the rules that will allow the distributors to achieve the top ranks. In many companies, distributors achieve the top ranks by creating ten to twenty first-level sales leaders. If a company creates a rule like this, its distributors will have to sponsor a lot of people in order to be achieve the top rank.

Section Two: The Building Blocks

On the Soapbox

One of the challenges I face as a consultant is to be shown this chart and be asked, "How much will it actually pay out?" Well, that's a little like forecasting a combination of the weather and the stock market a year in advance. However, if I know the commission plan rules to advance from 1-Star to 5-Star, I can tell a company what to expect. This payout can vary from ten percent to thirty percent, based on how easy it is for an individual distributor to achieve the higher levels of payout. In one instance, I was called back and told my payout projections were wrong, but when I reviewed the rules for rank advancement in their commission plan, I noticed that they had been made much easier. The company told me that the distributors had complained that qualifications were too hard. The company had forgotten that making it easier to advance would raise their payout. The payout of a commission plan is controlled as much by the rules as it is by the commission percentages.

	1-Star	2-Star	3-Star	4-Star	5-Star	
	5%	5%	5%	5%	5%	1st Level
	5%	5%	5%	5%	5%	2nd Level
		5%	5%	5%	5%	3rd Level
			5%	5%	5%	4th Level
				5%	5%	5th Level
					5%	6th Level

Once a company decides which qualifiers to use, the next question it must consider is whether a distributor must reach the qualifications to achieve a rank within a month or within several months, or whether those qualifications are going to accumulate forever. Here's a quick list of the pros and cons for each approach.

1 month – All the volume to achieve a certain rank has to be earned in one month.

- **Pros**:
  - Creates a sense of urgency and commitment.
  - Allows someone to advance more quickly.
  - Helps companies increase sales volume quickly.
- **Cons**:
  - Sometimes this is so tough to accomplish that the requirement drives away good leaders.
  - Can encourage front-end loading.
  - Can create frustration if the distributor misses qualification by very little and has to start over the next month.
  - Distributors often hold orders until they're sure they've met the requirement, thereby frustrating their consumers.

Multi-month – A distributor can accumulate volume to achieve a rank advancement over a several-month period.

- **Pros**:
  - Still some urgency, with less of a penalty if a distributor makes a mistake.
  - Encourages distributors to build a consistent business.
  - Rank advancement qualifications can be more closely matched up with monthly commission qualifications.
- **Cons**:
  - Companies tend to set much larger requirements, which can penalize fast growing distributorships.

Accumulative – A distributor can accumulate volume to achieve a rank advancement over any period of time.

- **Pros**:
  - Encourages building a loyal consumer base.
  - Least prone to front-end loading

- **Cons:**
    - The company has to protect the salespeople and be careful not to allow consumers to "eat their way" to the top rank.
    - Does not create any sense of urgency to "get it done."

Reversion

The next issue a company faces is: once the distributors achieve a rank, do they always have that rank? Or can they be reduced in rank if they don't maintain certain qualification? Reduction of rank is called "reversion." If a plan allows for reversion, the company must have a *rule* about how long a distributor can hold a rank without qualifying before they're reduced in rank.

Companies must consider this type of situation when building their commission plan. How long can a distributor carry a rank without qualifying? If the requirements are too strict, distributors may quit, or they might wind up with garages full of product. If the requirements are too lax, a company may wind up with an organization full of uncommitted leaders. A company must create just the right balance.

Some companies have implemented reversion rules that turned out to be far too severe. A distributor of several years might have a difficult few months, and a too-strict reversion rule might take him completely out of the tree, basically taking away his organization and forcing him to start over. Such rules can induce anxiety and anger rather than motivation. Another consideration is that applying compression to the payout process eliminates many of the effects on the upline commission payout that created the reasons for having a very strict reversion policy because it temporarily bypasses the unqualified distributors, thus improving the payout for the upline. Again, it's important to be balanced. Strict reversion rules have pretty much disappeared, and most companies now let unqualified distributors maintain rank for at least a few months before reverting them.

Another issue is: if they retain the rank, are they always paid at that rank, not paid at all, or is there a third option of allowing them to qualify to be paid at a lower rank than their permanent rank? It has become a common practice to allow a distributor to qualify to be paid commissions at a lower rank than their permanent higher rank.

On the Soapbox

CROSSING THE DESERT

When the pioneers headed to California in the days of the Old West, they came upon the huge deserts of Nevada, containing little water and no food. The deserts took days to cross. At the edge of the desert, they discarded anything they could, loaded up on water, and headed across as fast as they could, hoping to get across before they ran out of water and died.

What does that have to do with network marketing? In many successful companies, sales leaders have to "cross the desert." For a while, they have to work very hard to become a sales leader, but their efforts initially don't earn them enough to pay for the time, energy, and money they expend to reach that rank. Some people view that situation as bad, or even dishonest. I don't agree. Anyone who has gone to college has "crossed a desert," and twenty years of building software companies has certainly caused me to cross my own share of deserts.

But a company needs to understand the ramifications of having its distributors cross the desert to become leaders. If the process is extremely difficult and expensive, and if people are misled about the size of the desert or the reward that they will obtain on the other side, the people who try but fail can become very upset. They won't stay as consumers, and they'll tell everyone they know about their bad experience and point out that it was the company's fault.

What do companies do to make a new distributor cross the desert? Typically, "breakaway" plans cause the distributor to work very hard for a little reward to become a sales leader and gain a bigger reward later. Another desert would be if a distributor has very high personal or group sales requirements to qualify for a certain rank, and if he or she fails to qualify one month and as a result loses rank or even an entire downline.

On the Soapbox

Continued

The reason companies create these deserts to cross is simple. Sales leaders normally make ten to fifteen percent on their group sales. The easier it is to become a sales leader, the more people do it, and that leaves less income for each sales leader. So the secret is for companies to make the "desert" hard enough to cross that only those who are serious about the business will cross the desert, but not so hard that everyone dies along the way.

Monthly qualification rules

In most plans, monthly qualification rules determine the rank at which distributors are paid each month. A company can use the same types of qualifications that it uses for rank advancements. However, these requirements are typically lower than they were for achieving a rank.

In most companies, the lower ranks (in the example I've been using, these would be 1-Star through 3-Star) usually only have a couple of requirements: a personal volume requirement and possibly one or two others. Once a distributor achieves the rank of sales leader (4-Star), the requirements start to become more complex. In addition to personal volume, a group volume requirement is very common. Also, structure requirements start to become very common as well. How it defines group volume and the amount of the monthly group volume required for rank advancement is one of the most crucial decisions a company must make. If the group volume requirement is too low, the salesperson won't make enough money to make their distributorship economically viable. If the volume requirement is too high, the distributors can burn out, end up with garages full of product, and sell their excess product for ten cents on the dollar over the Internet.

In many plans, group volume is the base unit for paying sales management commissions, known as leader or generation commissions. These are the backbone of many commission plans. The amount a sales leader and dream-builder will earn in a plan is often as much a function of the size of the group volume requirement as it is the percentages paid on that group volume.

So what is an appropriate group volume requirement? The factors to take into account are:

1. How much product will the average family of consumers use in a month?
2. What percent of potential consumers are likely to purchase the products?
3. Is it a consumable product or a one-time sale?
4. How easy is it for distributors to breakaway and no longer be part of the group volume of their sponsor?

In a company with highly consumable products, group sales volume requirements of around twenty households of usage tend to work reasonably well. I've seen companies with qualifications as high as ninety households of usage, which seems to be too high. Salespeople couldn't sell that much product. In order to maintain their qualification, distributors ended up buying product they didn't need each month.

On the Soapbox

INTERNATIONAL PLANS

One challenge a company needs to keep in mind as it sets its personal, group, and downline qualification sales volumes is its international plans, since these qualifications are typically based on the amount of the company's product used by an average consumer. If a company expands to a country where the average income is substantially different, can it keep the same qualifications? If it changes qualifications in one country, but keeps them constant in another, how will that work? These items need to be thought through before a company embarks on international expansion.

Other rules to consider

Here are a few other rules that have been very effective in protecting both companies and distributors:

Product buyback: A few years ago, the Direct Selling Association (DSA, at www.dsa.org) instituted a policy that required its member companies to buy back any product purchased by distributors for one year and charge no more than a ten percent restocking fee. This great policy protects distributors. However, one way that distributors can abuse the policy is to purchase product to qualify for a commission and then return the product. To combat this abuse, most companies replace defective product only with new product or give the distributor a cash refund only if the distributor is terminating the distributorship. It seems harsh, but, as a practical matter, has worked out to be fair to both parties.

Changing sponsorship: Some companies allow a distributor to change his or her sponsor under certain circumstances. This policy is almost always a bad idea. It leads to downline poaching and counter-poaching, and the company ends up refereeing the situation. No matter what the company decides, someone is always mad at them. I've seen companies say, "We'll allow you to change sponsors if your upline isn't supporting you," but that's like when I get in the middle of a fight between two of my kids and ask, "Who started it?" Entire management teams can become 100 percent consumed by this problem. In the end, most companies stick with the policy that a distributor stays under the person who sponsored him. This rule allows management to spend their time doing what they're supposed to do: run the company.

Distributorship terminations: When distributors terminate their distributorships, most companies don't allow them to sign up again for between six months and one year. The reason for this rule is to prevent a distributor from terminating just to get around the changing sponsorship rule.

Only one distributor per household: Distributors often sponsor someone else in their household as a way to stack additional levels into their downline and pick up additional commissions, or to get around the sponsorship change rule. If the plan has effective anti-stacking mechanisms in place, this rule is probably not necessary. Sometimes a husband and wife travel in different circles, and so it may be justified to let them have separate distributorships.

Summary

It's amazing to me how often companies agonize endlessly over the details of the percentages of their commission plan and then just copy the rules from another company without much thought, never realizing that the rules make the plan. If you want to understand a commission plan, you must understand its rules. If you do not understand its rules, you do not understand the plan.

Understanding Multi-Level Commissions

Chapter Six

Key Topics

Reasons for structure requirements 112
Types of structure requirements. 114
   Required-width structure. 114
      Pros and Cons. 115
   Limited-width structure. 116
      Pros and Cons 116
   Sponsor/Enroller tree. 118
   Multiple business center tree 119
   Coding commissions 121
   Australian 2-up 122
Summary 122

Understanding Multi-Level Commissions

How does *structure* affect commission plans?

Structure has always caused heated debate among professional network marketers. Some people swear you should build wide; others say you should build deep; still others think you should build wide, so that you can build deep.

The structure components of commission plans have become very complex over the last twenty years. In this chapter, we will talk about six topics that relate to the structure component of commission plans:

1. *Required structure* - this is any commission plan requirement that requires that a distributor have a certain number of distributors organized in a certain manner in their downline.

2. *Limited structure* - this is any commission plan requirement that limits the number of distributors a person can have on their first level.

3. *Sponsors and enrollers* - this is an innovation that allows for two downline trees, part of the commission plan is paid based on each downline tree.

4. *Multi-center downline trees* – this is the practice of allowing a single distributor to have more than one position in a downline tree.

5. *Coding commission* - this commission locks in the upline ranks and structure as they are at the time a distributor is sponsored, so that some, or all, future commissions are forever paid based on those ranks and that structure.

6. *"Australian 2-up" distributor giveaway plans* - in these plans, every distributor gives up the first two distributors they sponsor to their upline.

Over the last twenty years, there have always been a few companies start up every year that, instead of focusing on commission types to make a commission plan work, focus on making the perfect downline structure instead. They rely on a relatively simple commission plan, typically a simple level commission. The four major variants of these plans have been the Matrix, Binary, Australian 2-up, and traditional plans that add some structural components like enroller trees or coding commissions.

The challenge the structure plans have faced is that it seems there is no one perfect way to build a downline organization. You can't develop a perfect 3X9 or 5X7 structure of leaders; you have to develop leaders where you find them. Some distributors have to recruit ten first-levels to find three good leaders; others only have to recruit three first-levels to find three good leaders. It depends on the leader and on a host of other issues.

So what are structure requirements? Any rule in a commission plan that requires a minimum number of distributors, qualified distributors, sales leaders, or qualified sales leaders in a distributor's downline or on a specific level of their downline. This is known as *required-width structure*. One type of structure requirement can help qualify a distributor for commission payments or even to retain the distributorship. A second type of structure only *allows* a certain number of distributors on each distributor's first level; this is known as *limited-width structure*. Although they're both structure requirements, they're as different as night and day in their effect on a commission plan.

Reasons for structure requirements

I'm often asked why companies have structure requirements for advancing to the top ranks in their commission plans. The plain and simple answer: requiring a minimum amount of structure is still the best way available to ensure that a leader builds a solid organization. If all requirements were simply based on downline volume, the same downline volume could qualify two or even ten or more people for the top ranks of a plan. But, of course, a company could not pay all of those people the same commission for the same sales volume. How would a company know whom to pay? The answer is: the one who actually built a solid downline, or the one with the proper downline *structure*.

Initially, leader commissions in traditional breakaway companies were only a few percent per level. After a while, however, the leaders began to want more; they wanted these percentages increased to reflect their hard work. Network marketing companies began to offer them an increased payout *if* the distributor would increase the size of their downline organizations. Downline structure and sales volume became the two ways of defining how much distributors had to build their organizations in order to receive the additional commissions. Companies were effectually saying, "If you build an additional downline leg in your organization, we'll give you five percent on your fourth level."

In the "new unilevels" of the 1980s, structure was the primary weapon in the war against stacking. If the company required a distributor to have three legs in his organization, each with a certain specified level of volume, it was difficult to stack. If the company had no structural requirements, a distributor could stack levels between himself and the bulk of his organization, so none of the commission would go to his upline, who recruited and trained him.

But with a structure requirement, the distributor has to build a solid organization to earn commissions. So how does a structure requirement help? If you look at Figure 15, each person from A through E has a million dollars of downline sales volume. But who should receive the majority of the commissions for building this million-dollar business? Most people would agree that person E has built the strongest organization, and the way the company would know that person E is the one to pay is because it can see by the structure of the organization that person E did all the business.

Figure 15

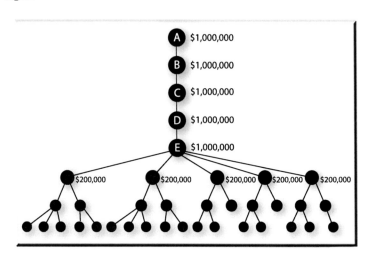

Types of structure requirements

As I mentioned earlier, in terms of structure for network marketing companies, there are two different methodologies. *Required-width* structures require that distributors must have *at least* a certain number of people first level to them. *Limited-width* structures specify that distributors *can't* have more than a certain number of people first level to them.

Required-width structure.

Required structures serve two purposes. One is that they're a good component in an anti-stacking policy. The other is these requirements offer concrete steps that distributors can strive for as they work to achieve higher ranks. For example, to tell someone he needs to generate $100,000 a month in sales is too general and sometimes seems like too much to bite off all at once. However, telling that recruit to find three people who can each find three, who can find three to do $2,500 in group volume might sound more reasonable, even though that also adds up to $100,000 in sales volume.

Pros and Cons.

Required structure in and of itself is almost universal among successful network marketing companies. However, it's important to remember to keep the requirements reasonable. Years ago, we'd see requirements for thirty first-level sales leaders to reach the top rank of a company. In practice, that is almost impossible. Now most companies limit the number of required first-level sales leaders to a smaller number and combine it with other the requirements we discussed in Chapter Five. This approach allows the sales leader flexibility. They can build lots of first-level leaders or can build deep with fewer first level leaders.

Two other types of requirements are very difficult and seem to cause great frustration with distributors. One is what I call "the perfect structure". These requirements are very tough. If the organization goes three levels deep, the distributor needs thirty-nine distributors perfectly organized. If one of those distributors becomes unqualified, they have to be replaced in exactly that position in the downline, and that is very tough!

Figure 16

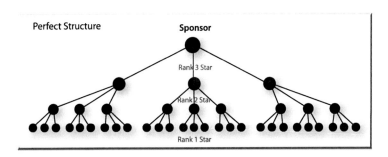

Second, some companies have a requirement that once its distributors reach the top rank, they have to build a new downline leg every year. The problem is that takes leaders away from working with their existing downlines to build a new leg from scratch. At some point sales leaders need to have the option to work their existing business where it has the most potential to grow and with the leaders they already have in place. I understand that companies want to keep sales leaders working, but this method has proven to cause great difficulty.

Required structure in a plan is a good thing. Most plans have some required structure built into them in order to be workable. Otherwise, the organization doesn't have a solid foundation.

Limited-width structure.

The structures in some commission plans limit the width of an individual's downline. In other words, a distributor can't have an unlimited number of first-level distributors directly beneath him or her in the tree. This limitation is limited-width structure, sometimes called forced structure or forced matrix.

There are two types of limited width structure plans: matrix and binary. A *binary* is a limited-width matrix that only allows two first levels, but uses a different kind of commission than any other kind of matrix. A *matrix* limits the number of first levels, but usually allow more than two first levels and normally pays a level commission type.

The payout attributes of the binary are so different that I talk about it separately in Chapter Ten when I discuss commission plans.

Pros and Cons

The initial selling points of matrix were that, because no one could have more than a certain number of first levels, "your upline would help build your downline." In other words, once your upline had sponsored more than they could have on their first level, the additional distributors they sponsored would "spillover" into your downline. Most of the original matrixes had the computer software automatically place the "spillover" distributors in the distributor's downline

The second big selling point of matrix was that some distributors could not steal all the good distributors by sponsoring them all; they had to "share the wealth."

The last selling point of this type of plan is the same selling point as the unilevel it's designed to replace. It's simple and easy to understand.

What are the challenges inherent in limited-width structure? Because of the focus on structure, distributors get very concerned about how their organization looks. For example, I used to get letters and emails asking for the most efficient ways to fill in the structure. This is not something to worry about; they should be worrying about making sales. Another concern is if the distributor or the software makes an error in placing someone in the tree, you can't move that person. That error can never be solved because other distributors are being place under him, and then it becomes like trying to unscramble an egg. The error becomes serious if that leg is growing. This problem is most serious with binary plans, but it occurs in all structure-based plans.

It also promotes a welfare mentality. The idea was "I'll wait for my upline to build my downline." But there was not a lot of spillover in the companies I provided the software for, because it seems distributors who sponsored lots of distributors did not join matrixes. They instead joined companies that rewarded distributors for sponsoring lots of distributors. So there was lots of disappointment.

The original matrix plans had no strategy for paying sales commissions to salespeople. Some of the later plans added the concept of sponsor/enroller trees, and with the enroller tree, they paid sales commissions and that helped that problem. Binary has always been the exception here, because its commission type is so different. It has always done a good job of paying salespeople.

Limited-width structure has always been a challenge. In matrix plans, it's hard to find a lot of success. In the binary world, Market America and Usana are the big-name successes, although several new companies are doing quite well as binary hybrids, combining the binary plan with other commission types. It seems to me these companies have done well where others have failed by doing what must be done in all plans: working around the limitations and taking advantage of the strengths. But above all, they do not promise that the commission plan itself will work miracles.

Understanding Multi-Level Commissions

Sponsor/Enroller tree

The concept of two downline trees, a "sponsor" tree and an "enroller" tree, started in the late 1980s as part of the forced matrix commission plan boom. As companies worked through the challenges caused by this new commission plan, one problem kept coming up over and over again. In a matrix plan, a distributor did not have an incentive to sponsor a lot of first-level distributors. If it was a 3X9 plan, there was not much incentive to sponsor more than three distributors. So companies needed to come up with a way to get their best recruiters back to work. The result was the sponsor/enroller system. The first downline was a forced matrix "sponsor" downline that only allowed three first levels, and the second was an "enroller" downline that allowed as many first levels as a person enrolled. The company then paid part of the commissions through the sponsor downline and part of the commissions through the enroller downline.

The concept worked pretty well and had only one real problem. It increased the complexity of the commission plan. The company had to maintain two downline genealogies, and the distributors had to monitor two downlines. But there were significant benefits as well—benefits that companies not using the forced matrix plan could also utilize.

By the late 1990s, the Internet was firmly entrenched in the network marketing arena, giving distributors instant access to their downline information. This made some of the problems of maintaining two genealogies less of a problem. It also increased the amount of long-distance sponsoring that occurred. Long-distance sponsoring often benefits from a sponsor/enroller program. If I live on the East coast and I sponsor someone on the West coast, I may want to actually have that person sponsored by someone geographically closer, but list myself as the enroller so that I receive some benefit. As a result of these and other such situations, sponsor/enroller programs have also become quite popular with companies that don't use any type of matrix plan.

How do sponsor/enroller trees work? They're actually quite simple. The company sets up a sponsor downline and an enroller downline, and selects one or more commission types that are paid for each downline. The important part is that a company has to decide which commissions are paid to enrollers and which are paid to sponsors. These payment policies need to be consistent.

Multiple business center tree

This fairly simple concept got its start in the structure plans of the early 1980s. A multiple business center tree allows a distributor to have several positions in the downline tree.

Multi-center trees are implemented in two ways. In the original version, once distributors succeed in filling in their original matrix, they can have a new business center in the tree and build a new downline from that center. This method was set up to keep people from having their earnings capped when their original matrix was mostly filled, and the business center was placed several levels deep in the distributors original organization. In the second method, all of the business centers are created at the time the distributor is sponsored, and the distributor's entire downline is placed under these multiple business centers. From the distributor's standpoint, this system is better because it allows them to receive multiple commission checks on their *entire* downline. It's essentially company-endorsed stacking.

This second form of multiple business centers became standard with the original binary commission plans. When the original binary plans were designed, a single business center could not earn more than $1,500 per week. With such restrictions on income, most dreambuilders were hesitant to become involved. Distributors were allowed to choose one, three, or seven business centers or, in some binary plans, even more. Now instead of being limited to $1,500 per week, a distributor had an earnings potential $1,500 times seven business centers or $10,500 per week.

Companies liked the plan because a distributor was required to generate a certain sales volume for each business center. That requirement guaranteed so much in product sales per year per business center. Since it was impossible for distributors to add business centers after they started to build their business, many distributors signed up with seven business centers "just in case."

At this point, the scams got involved and added multiple business centers purchased at the time a distributor signed up to traditional matrix plans such as 3x9 and 5x7. These organizations would let a distributor buy as many business centers as he wanted. But the distributor had to pay between $400 and $1,000 for each business center.

How far did this multi-center mania go? Our software initially accommodated only nine business centers for a distributor. We later expanded that number to 99. One company that considered purchasing our software required that it accommodate up to 10,000 business centers for a single distributor. I asked if they really expected anyone to buy this many, and they replied that one distributor had already purchased over a thousand business centers, at a total cost of close to a million dollars!

I talked to several industry attorneys and changed our software so that it no longer supports more than nine business centers. I have never seen any business justification for more business centers than that.

On the Soapbox

One of the difficult things about the industry and commissions is the terminology. There is a passage in Genesis that talks about the Tower of Babel that I jokingly apply to this situation. *"Go to, let us go down, and there confound the language, that they may not understand one another's speech"*. In my dealings with many different companies, distributors, and consultants, I have found that many times one person is using one term to mean one thing and another person is using a different term. Talk about not being able to understand each other! It obviously creates great confusion. Here are a couple of examples. I already discussed how people confuse the terms "rollup" and "compression". Recently, companies are using the term "coding commission" to define what I know as Australian 2-up. I don't know what these companies would call a coding commission. Even after twenty years in the industry, there are times when I simply have to hand someone a piece of paper and tell them to draw what they are talking about, and then I can say "Oh, you mean…".

Coding commissions

Coding commissions are used with differential and sometimes level commissions. The concept seems deceptively simple. The idea is that when a distributor is sponsored, the ranks and structure of that person's upline is "coded." From that point on, the upline is paid on that distributor's personal sales based on this coded rank and structure. Simple, right? Wrong. Coding commissions are extremely difficult to make work for several reasons:

1. Mistakes. Sometimes people make mistakes and those codes are set wrong, distributors are entered in the wrong order, or in the wrong spot. The distributor's rank advancement doesn't happen until after a top distributor is entered and this permanent code is set wrong. It can make people very unhappy.

2. Timing. If you sponsor your best salesperson when you first start out in the business, that individual is coded to you when you're still at a low rank. You can never make any more money on his or her sales than is allowed for the low rank. You do however make more money on the distributors they sponsor. Many people don't realize this and get very frustrated.

If you ask ten people what a coding commission is, you will probably get ten different answers. It hasn't been widely used, and its behavior is not well understood by distributors. And there's nothing distributors dislike more than being surprised at commission time. Therefore, any company that uses a coding commission needs to make sure the distributors understand what to expect.

So what is the benefit? Some companies have had good success with a coding commission because they spent the time to educate their distributors about the benefits and how the commission works. Therefore, no one was surprised at commission time.

Understanding Multi-Level Commissions

Australian 2-up

This commission plan has to win the prize for the most interesting plan ever devised by sober people, assuming they were sober. The basic idea is that everyone gives up the first two distributors they sponsor to their sponsor. Assuming all distributors are the same, this is a fine plan. The distributor gives up two distributors and gets four in return. Those four each give you the first two distributors they sponsor, so you get another eight, those eight give up the first two they sponsor so you get another sixteen....

So what's the downside? Distributors are *not* all the same. Up to seventy percent of distributors do not sponsor anyone, so if the two a distributor is given by her first level fall in this category, she is not very happy. And only a few sponsor more than five. If a distributor's first level gives up one of those few distributors who sponsors more than five, he is not very happy to have given up a great distributor. And if the company makes a data entry error so that the wrong person is given up, then the distributors can be very unhappy with the company. That's a lot of potential for unhappiness.

The commission types used by Australian 2-ups are generally level commissions. The only real success for this plan was a company name Eagle Shield in the late 1980s.

Summary

One of the difficulties in creating a commission plan that's built around certain structure is that it's critical that data be entered absolutely correctly. It can't be entered and then corrected later like you can do with most data. However, now that some network marketing companies are receiving as much as ninety percent of their orders and distributor applications through the Internet, the distributors themselves are taking responsibility for making sure the data is correct.

This has allowed some of the concepts in structured plans, like the enroller tree and binary tree, to become more popular over time, as innovative companies work out some of the challenges and create some real benefits for the distributors.

Chapter Seven

Key Topics

Overview 125
Matching Commissions 125
Automobile Shared Pool Commissions 126
Fast-start commissions 129
Incentive Programs 130
Summary 131

Understanding Multi-Level Commissions

What are the other miscellaneous commissions a company can utilize?

Overview

This is a rather broad topic for a chapter. These commissions are so diverse that I call the chapter "miscellaneous" commissions, but they're still important to discuss. The matching, automobile, and fast start commissions are sort of like dessert to a meal. You can live without it, but, in some cases, it's what makes the meal appealing. I typically recommend that companies not rely solely on these commissions for the backbone of their plan.

Matching Commissions

The term *matching commissions* refers to a system that pays distributors a percentage of the *earnings* of the people in their organizations rather than paying a percentage based on personal or group sales, as in the other commissions. Matching is a type of level commission. Matching commissions can be paid on either the sponsor tree or the enroller tree.

A company can add matching commissions to almost any plan. In some plans, it makes the most sense for distributors to place the new people they sponsor down in the organization, where they may not earn as much, because of a need to meet certain group volume or downline leg requirements. Doing so may put them out of a distributor's payline. Companies may use a matching commission to compensate distributors and to continue to motivate them to recruit new people.

When we say matching commissions it means that the company matches a percentage of one or more of the commission types. For example, a company may have a level commission and is paying a 10 percent matching commission to the enroller. If a distributor earns $1,000, this distributor's enroller would earn $100. Typically the company does not pay a matching commission on the matching commission a distributor earns.

Automobile Shared Pool Commissions

These commissions have been a staple in network marketing since the 1970s. The most famous car program in direct sales history is Mary Kay's pink Cadillac. In fact, the branding that Mary Kay associates with the pink Cadillac is so strong that General Motors actually has a shade of pink specifically branded for Mary Kay.

Why do companies create car programs? The first reason is that it turns their distributors into walking (actually driving) billboards. The car can also be a powerful reward for a distributor who has "crossed the desert" and become a sales leader.

Another reason is to create the perception that the distributor is earning more money. Instead of paying a distributor $1,000 per month, a company can pay $500 per month and give the distributor $500 per month for a payment on a car. Now, when that distributor's friends ask what he makes in his little side business, he can say, "About $500 a month, but the company also gives me that new Acura." In some people's minds, that adds up to more than $1,000.

This method of reward is especially powerful because getting a new luxury car is one of the signs that you've made it. You're a success. You might ask, "What's the definition of a luxury car?" In this context, it seems it's any car that's a step up from what the distributor's friends drive. If they all drive used cars, it's any new car. If they drive $15,000 cars, it's a $30,000 car, and so on.

The last major reason for a car incentive program is the sense of commitment to the company it encourages in distributors. If working their business earns them the money that pays for a new car that impresses everyone they know, that's a powerful incentive.

Technically, how do these programs work? There are two primary methods. The first method has been around for a long time. The company buys or leases the car, and the distributor earns part or all of the payment based on defined performance criteria. If sales performance drops below certain levels, the distributor no longer is entitled to the car. This is where this method can create a problem. What happens when the distributor no longer qualifies for the car? The company has to repossess it. Not surprisingly, people don't like it when you repossess their car. All the work the company has done to make the distributor feel part of the family can be pretty much blown away.

The advantage to this method is that it's simple and hassle free for the distributor. She either qualifies for the car or doesn't. If she does qualify, the car shows up on her doorstep. You will notice that the explanation of the other method of automobile program is significantly more complex.

One of the reasons companies started running the program this way because getting a car loan used to be much more difficult than it is today, especially for self-employed people. But now that the automobile manufacturers offer attractive financing programs, this problem is mostly gone.

Today there is a second method of automobile programs. They're actually pool commissions.

There are two types of these car programs generally used today. One is quite simple. If a company has ranks of 1-Star through 9-Star. When the distributor achieves the 5-Star rank, he or she receives a certain dollar amount car commission, say $300, in any month that he or she is qualified. When they achieve the 6-Star rank, the car commission might go to $500 per month, and so on as the distributor advances in rank.

The second form of car commission is more complex. Distributors who qualify for the car program decide what car they want, then fill out a form that determines the amount they qualify for. For example, a company might take the price of the car, plus twenty percent for interest and taxes, plus a certain percentage for maintenance, and then divide that number by 36 months. That amount determines the maximum payment the distributor can receive every month. Qualifying distributors send in the calculation, proof of purchase, and a photo of themselves and their new cars. The actual amount they receive is determined by some formula. There are rules, for example, about how a distributor earns "car points." Each dollar of group sales volume is one point, each dollar of first-generation sales volume is half a point, each dollar of second-generation sales volume is a quarter of a point, and so on. At the end of the month, the company adds up all the points earned by all the distributors and divides it by the amount the company has designated for the car program.

The company normally sets aside one or two percent of sales to fund the car program. This amount determines the value of each point. Then for each distributor, they multiply the point value by the number of points the distributor received. The company may have other rules that cover what to do if the distributor earns less than the maximum and how they can make it up later when they earn more than the monthly maximum.

The strong points of this type of a program are:

- The company never has to repossess the car;
- Distributors can actually buy more expensive cars than they qualify for and have their commissions grow into it;
- The car leases are not liabilities for the company;
- It's easy to administer;
- The photos are great for the company to post on their "hall of fame."

The pros and cons of the two approaches are pretty obvious. The first type of program is simple, and distributors like that. The second type of program allows distributors to earn more money as their downline grows, and distributors also like that.

The only real negative about the second type of car program is that if a company sets up its point system so that the new leaders can get enough points to get a car, sooner or later, the top distributors will be getting enough points to get several thousand dollars a month toward a car. But not many cars cost that much. Then the company gets pressure to allow them to use "their" money for more and more things: homes, vacations, boats, and so forth. This problem leads to devaluing the point so that new leaders can no longer qualify for enough money for a car.

Section Two: The Building Blocks

Fast-start commissions

These commissions have come into their own over the last few years. Commissions can be unilevel, stepped infinity, or coded. The concept is that when a distributor signs someone up, certain products, product packs, or the first certain amount of product they buy are paid not under the standard commission plan, but rather under a different commission plan. The purpose is to get higher sales commissions to the upline on the first few sales to someone new in the program. (see Figure 17 for the difference between a standard unilevel plan and a fast-start unilevel plan)

Figure 17

More money goes to the sponsor and less goes to the upline on each new recruit's sales. A distributor can earn fast start commission each time they recruit someone for as long as he or she is in the company, but it's only paid for the first few months or for a certain amount of each recruit's sales volume.

Another variation is for the company to pay half of the new recruit's volume under the fast start and half under the standard plan.

The advantage of the fast start is that it not only gives sponsors incentive to work with the new distributors to build their business, but also gives them incentive to work quickly because they receive this commission for only a limited time; three months is common.

The disadvantage of fast start is that if someone comes in and recruits a lot of people in the first three months, in the fourth month their commission can drop by as much 75 percent as these recruits move back to the normal plan. This drop in income can be very discouraging. The distributors seem to feel that the company has taken something away, rather than feeling that the company gave them something extra for three months. A commission plan can solve this problem somewhat by having the fast start phase out over time rather than abruptly end.

Another disadvantage is that in some plans, after the three-month period, the amount a distributor makes on a consumer can be so little that it no longer makes economic sense to spend time taking care of the customer. Additionally, fast start is open to some forms of manipulation. Distributors, for example, can put all of their volume under their new distributors in order to receive the higher percentage.

Creating big-paying, fast-start commissions has not proven to create long-term growth. A moderate fast start can work well, but if a company makes it so easy that it generates a lot of extra commissions, distributors seem to remember the negative feeling generated by the loss all of those commissions long after they've forgotten the positive feeling of getting the money originally.

Incentive Programs

Money isn't the only thing that motivates people. This was what Napoleon was talking about when he said, "Give me enough ribbon and I will conquer all of Europe." Companies can create recognition, cash contests, and trips. A company can have these incentives computed, tracked, and reported on the monthly commission statements.

As a company works to create a loyal distributor force, it's important to remember that for distributors who are earning a few hundred dollars a month, a free trip to a convention can be the trip of a lifetime. As companies design contests, it's important to remember the five types of distributors. Contests can be much more targeted to specific distributor types than commissions can.

Other ideas, such as buy one get one free, free shipping, new product promos, and product credit are also very successful.

In the late 1990s, when many traditional network marketing companies were having flat sales, many party plan companies were doing very well. The areas of contests and incentives are areas where party plans companies traditionally excel. This has caused many of their network marketing cousins to take a look at what the party plan companies are doing so they can improve. The area of incentives is certainly one of those areas.

Summary

As you can see from the commissions discussed in this chapter, there are some great ways to create additional value for the distributor. It's important, however, that a company remember that these commissions are added after the commission strategy is defined, and typically after the majority of the commission plan is designed.

Understanding Multi-Level Commissions

Chapter Eight

Key Topics

Overview 135
Pricing... 135
Reduced commission value products 137
International Commissions................................ 138
Open Enrollment vs. Barriers-to-Signup 141
Open enrollment 141
Barriers to signup 144

Understanding Multi-Level Commissions

Section Two: The Building Blocks

What are the operational issues a network marketing company faces?

Overview

In this chapter, we will discuss some important issues that you might not think would affect the commission plan, but they do. I refer to the pricing methodologies a company adopts, the method a company chooses for doing business internationally, and whether it adopts an open-enrollment or barriers-to-signup strategy of recruiting distributors.

Pricing

The pricing of a company's product line has a lot to do with its commission plan. There are a lot of issues that have to be considered, and everything about the commission plan flows from these decisions. Who are the distributors going to market the product to? This is important because network marketing is *peer-to-peer marketing,* so the plan must be attractive to the target audience. Does the product take a long time to train people to use? Is it consumable? Is the answer yes for some products and no for other products the company sells? These are the questions to which you must know the answers. As a general rule, the harder it is to train consumers to use a product, the higher the commission percentage you should anticipate on the sale of the product. A higher commission should also be paid on a more expensive product. On consumable or easy-to-understand products, commissions can be less.

As we discussed earlier, most companies pay total commissions of between thirty-five and fifty percent of the "distributor price" of the product. If a company pays less than that, it's difficult to be competitive. If a company pays more than that, it's difficult to have a good quality product and afford to stay in business and be competitive.

Most successful companies ultimately publish a price list that looks like this:

Understanding Multi-Level Commissions

Figure 18

Item Code	Country	Item Name	Distributor Price	Suggested Retail	Commission Value (CV)	Qualifying Points (QP)
1235	USA	Product 1	$100.00	$150.00	$100.00	$100.00
1235	Canada	Product 1	$120.00	$160.00	$120.00	$100.00

Many distributors and company executives do not like this price list because it's too complex; however, let's look at why so many companies end up using it.

Commission Value (CV) is the price that commissions are calculated from. In many companies, the CV price is the same as the price that distributors pay for the product. And this is certainly what most distributors want companies to do; it's simple and easy to understand. However, it makes sense to list CV separately on the price list because it gives the company flexibility in the products it can sell. This is because even if the CV price is the same on nine out of ten products, a company needs flexibility to be able to show that tenth item correctly on the price list.

Qualifying Points (QP) This is how much a product counts towards the qualification requirements of a commission plan. Here again, it's often the same amount as the price of the product. However, if a company is doing business in multiple countries, and they allow distributors to sponsor downline distributors in multiple countries, then qualifications can't be expressed in dollars because other countries don't use dollars. The qualifications must be expressed in points. If a company is planning on doing business in more that one country, it should use qualifying points. Another advantage is that a company can increase or decrease QP independently from the price as a separate part of their marketing strategy.

Companies don't always use the terms CV and QP. They may use terms like SV, QV, PV or others. But the concept is still the same. As you can see, this type of pricing mechanism allows for the flexibility that any long-term company needs.

Now let's talk about the challenges of using this type of a pricing system.

Reduced commission value products

One of the great conveniences of this pricing method is that it allows companies to lower the commission value of a product, but leave the price the same. This means that the company will pay less commission on the product but sell it for the same price. In some cases, this is perfectly legitimate. Sometimes, in order to fill out its product line, a company wants to sell a product that doesn't have enough of a margin to pay full commission. It therefore has a lower CV on that one product. But in other cases, companies lower the CV on an entire range of products, or in some cases the entire product line. This action frustrates and confuses distributors because they feel that the rules are being changed in the middle of the game.

A second variation of the CV system occurs when all products have commission value that is significantly less than the price the distributor pays. One method that has been tried several times over the last twenty years is to make the commission percentages of the commission plan add up to 100 percent, while the CV on the price list is about thirty-five to fifty percent of the distributor price. There's nothing technically wrong with this idea. In the end, the money paid out ends up being the same as if the CV were 100 percent and the commission percentages were thirty-five to fifty percent. However, in my experience it's very confusing to distributors because it's so different from the traditional method of operation. In addition, so many companies have lowered CV as a method to reduce commissions that it immediately makes distributors suspicious.

Many companies end up needing to lower CV on a few products to fill out the product line. While distributors may be a little wary of it, this first method has worked But a second method of lowering CV across the board causes companies to deal with a lot of confused and frustrated distributors for a long time, so I would not recommend doing this.

International Commissions

Some companies have a ten-year plan to move into other countries. That's fine, but distributors will push their company to implement their plans much sooner. The reasons are quite simple.

First, network marketing is popular in many countries around the world. In fact, it's more popular elsewhere than in the United States, and several companies we've dealt with have established sales of popular products quickly and inexpensively. Obviously, international growth is profitable for a distributor's bottom line.

Second, one of the traditional major marketplaces for direct sales and network marketing is first- and second-generation immigrants who are ignored by mainstream corporate America. The reason is that these groups, even though there may be a few million in a community, are too small for mass media advertising. So as a network marketing company sells product into these ethnic groups, it's natural for those people to want share the product with their relatives. They send some to their home country for personal use, and then the pressure starts to build for a company to open business in that country.

It's interesting that often one of the first questions asked of my company is, "Can you pay international commissions?" The answer is yes, we've been paying commissions internationally for more than fifteen years. This assurance is often followed by a great sigh of relief, after which the clients tell us they're opening ten countries in the next year. Then we have to tell them that paying international commissions is the easy part of opening ten countries. Dealing with the international equivalents of the FDA and the IRS is the difficult and expensive part. Remember, these issues are complex and time-consuming, and this discussion is just an overview. A great deal of planning and preparation needs to go into any decision to move a company into the international market.

There are three major schools of thought on international commission plans. They are:

1. Single Worldwide Downline Unified Commission Plan: In this model, the plan is "seamless" worldwide. If I am a distributor

in the United States and sign up a distributor in the United Kingdom, it should not make any difference in commissions. The plan is the same throughout the world, and a distributors downline sales volume counts exactly the same regardless of where it comes from.

2. Single Downline/Regionalized Plan: In the United States, the GDP is $35,000 per person, and in Vietnam, the GDP is $2,000 per person. Remember in Chapter Five, we talked about the importance of personal and group sales requirements. They should be based on the number of consumers needed to meet these requirements. Proponents of this theory argue that if sales volume requirements are the same, then it's seventeen times as hard to meet them in Vietnam. These companies support a worldwide integrated downline, but argue that you can't have the exact same plan for both of these countries; the commission plan has to have regional or country differences. A distributor must qualify in his or her home region, but get paid on the entire world.

3. Separate Downlines/Separate Commission Plans: People who favor this approach argue that the problems caused by the regionalized scenario are so great that the notion of a worldwide downline simply can't work. They also contend that so few distributors actually build downlines outside of their home country that it's simply too expensive to justify.

Which is the best approach? Up until about fifteen years ago, it was so expensive to do unified commission plans that it simply was not done. And even when companies first started opening foreign offices, they tended to be in very well-to-do, high-GDP countries, and so the unified commission seemed to be well on its way to becoming the universal standard international plan. However, with the rapid explosion of the Internet in the last five years, it has become cost-effective for companies to open smaller countries with low GDP per person. Many companies have had to think long and hard about what they want to do.

At first, distributors in large markets almost universally like the first approach, which works well if the GDP per person is relatively the same in all countries where the company does business. But inevitably, distributors pressure companies to start opening countries where there is a large disparity between the GDP per person. That tends to be a bit of a challenge. You may remember that we talked earlier about the fact that one of the most important things to take into account when designing a commission plan is the socio-economic profile of a distributor. If the profiles vary greatly from country to country, a company tends to lean more toward the second method; however, not many companies have used that model. Consequently, many details are still unknown.

Then there is another issue that must be considered and that is the legal environment in a country. For example in Korea, it's against the law to pay more than thirty-five percent in commissions. If a company's plan pays more than thirty-five percent overall, then they cannot have a truly seamless worldwide plan. Most countries are going to have laws which a company will have to take into consideration, so a completely seamless plan is probably out of the question if the company is in more than a few countries.

The last concern involves computer costs. It's more expensive to process worldwide commissions than to process each country locally. Relatively few distributors sponsor internationally, but those few distributors can be the reason a newly opened country has such rapid growth in sales. The question is, who bears the additional computer costs—the distributors who sponsor internationally, all distributors, the company home office, or the individual offices in each country? These are questions that every company must answer before it embarks on an international business policy, because to debate them after the company has started paying international commissions is extremely difficult.

In summary, international sponsoring and commissioning has been the vehicle of success for some of the biggest network marketing companies in the industry today. It's certainly a part of the future of the industry, but each company has to determine its own way because no consensus has been reached on these issues. A discussion of international issues should be part of the commission plan development so as not to limit a company's options later.

Open Enrollment vs. Barriers-to-Signup

There are two basic methods for creating a network marketing company's sales force. They are:

1. Open enrollment. This strategy makes it easy and inexpensive to become and remain a distributor. Almost all people who become regular consumers of the company's product become "distributors" so that they can buy at "distributor wholesale." In this type of company, all commissions are paid within the commission plan. Very little retail commission is ever earned because most people become distributors.

2. Barriers-to-signup. In this strategy, only people committed to becoming active salespeople sign up as distributors. The company maintains this strategy by creating such barriers as an expensive product demonstration kit, required ongoing training, and high monthly personal sales requirements. In these companies, retail consumers are a reality, and the distributors receive the retail markup from product sales.

Both of these strategies have worked well over the years, The trouble comes when a company tries to mix and match the methods. They pick one method and then try to copy elements from a company using the other method. The decision as to which of these two methods to use is one of the first a company will make as it starts to create its commission plan. This chapter is a discussion of the benefits of each method, what a company gets by choosing that method, and what they give up.

Open enrollment

Let's begin with the open-enrollment strategy. Open enrollment is the staple of modern network marketing companies that have been around since the early 1980s.

The first item to note is that very little product is sold at retail price in an open enrollment company. Since by definition it's easy to become a distributor, if a person is going to become a regular consumer, they soon realize that it's cheaper to purchase a sales kit and

Understanding Multi-Level Commissions

throw it away and get the "distributor wholesale price" than continue to pay retail price. Now, are these people still consumers? Absolutely, and they still need to be treated as consumers or, in many cases, they will ultimately leave. Companies must realize this, and make sure that they pay the actual salespeople enough sales commission within the commission plan to service these consumers, because they can't rely on the retail markup.

There are certainly advantages to this strategy. One is that the consumers are dealing directly with the company. Therefore, the company knows who their consumers are. This can be a tremendous advantage over barrier-to-signup companies that often have no idea who their consumers are. In such a case, if a salesperson quits the business, the company loses all of that distributor's consumers.

A second advantage is that the company can help share the burden of consumer service. Yet a third advantage that has appeared over the last seven years is Internet ordering. This method lowers a company's costs and allows the company to provide better service to the customers.

In the open enrollment strategy, it's important that the plan fairly compensate the salesperson inside the sales plan. Often, when a new distributor signs up, the company must recognize that he may never sponsor anyone and the only thing he plans to do is buy product for his own consumption. In the upline of this consumer is someone who must fulfill the role of salesperson. Sometimes, the sponsor is the salesperson, but often the sponsor is a product evangelist and the salesperson is further upline. This salesperson provides the consumer service, explains the product, and fulfills the role of the traditional salesperson. In the upline of the salesperson is someone who has to fulfill the role of sales leader, managing the salesperson. The plan must be designed to compensate the salespeople and sales leaders for the extra time they must spend to service the distributors who are actually consumers.

Another advantage of this method is that the recruiting distributor doesn't have to try to determine what role someone is able to achieve with the company when signing that person up. For example, sometimes you recruit a distributor thinking he or she will be a sales leader, but instead that person ends up being a consumer. The reverse is also true; you think a new signup will only be a consumer, but instead that person ends up being one of your best sales leaders. In a properly designed open enrollment company, it doesn't matter if the distributor remains a consumer; the upline is nevertheless paid sales commission. If at some point, this consumer starts building a business, a well-designed commission plan will automatically adjust and start splitting the commissions, ultimately giving the entire commission to this new salesperson.

This point leads to the last advantage: the simplicity of the recruiting strategy. Many distributors like the fact that they have only one sales pitch and one form for people to fill out. With barriers-to-signup companies, distributors essentially have two sales pitches: one for consumers and a second for people they're signing up as distributors.

Now let's talk about some disadvantages of the open-enrollment strategy. First, it's much harder to get the design right in an open enrollment plan, and if you get them wrong, it's a much bigger problem. The plan must pay the salesperson to service the consumer. For example, if a plan pays only five percent for taking care of the consumers and the average product costs $30, a salesperson receives only $1.50 a month. Is someone going to adequately service a consumer for $1.50 per month? Many times the salespeople leave consumers to take care of themselves. Of course, consumers don't take care of themselves. They expect to be taken care of. Neglected consumers tend to leave.

Companies adopting this strategy with the wrong plan tend to be like grass fires: very hot on the edge (newly sponsored "consumers" buying product) and cold in the middle (older consumers no longer buying product). Consumers get excited and enthusiastic about the product, but then grow cool. They don't get their questions answered, they don't have contact from the company, or they run out of product. As one person put it, when they run out of product, they're *really* going to buy it the first day, they're *probably* going to buy it the second day, they think about *maybe* buying it on the third day, and then, by the fourth day, they *don't remember* it at all. People need to be sold. An open-enrollment strategy strongly depends on a strong sales commission strategy that compensates salespeople for taking care of their consumers. Many open-enrollment companies over the last few years have failed to provide such plans.

The second challenge of the open-enrollment strategy is the sheer numbers of distributors a company has to deal with, often three or four times as many as their barriers to signup cousins. These numbers can be overwhelming. My company had a client that had almost two million "distributors" on their computer. How do you deal with two million distributors? Companies need sophisticated computer systems and still have to spend a lot of time and energy to sort out the consumers, product evangelists, salespeople, sales leaders, and dreambuilders. They need to create marketing campaigns targeted to these different types of distributors. Unfortunately, many times, companies lack the computer systems and/or the ability to do the research and create targeted campaigns for the different types of distributors.

Overall, the open-enrollment strategy is gaining market share due in large part to the Internet revolution. It allows companies to deal efficiently with the masses of people and share the burden of servicing the consumer with the salesperson. Barriers-to-signup is certainly not dead, however. In fact, some of the fastest growing network marketing companies of the last five years have been barriers-to-signup companies. So let's talk about them.

Barriers to signup

What are barriers to signup? In a company where you want to keep consumers from becoming distributors and limit distributorships to those people who are actually going to sell your product, a company can create barriers that make it unattractive for a consumer to sign up as a distributor. Common barriers are:

1. Relatively expensive sales kits: for example, a several hundred dollar product demonstration kit that every distributor must purchase.

2. Required training: a consumer isn't willing to spend the time and money to go through this training.

Section Two: The Building Blocks

3. Monthly or quarterly retail sales requirements: A distributor is required to sell more products every month than a consumer could consume on his own. (Note that this is different from front-end loading or garage qualifying, which is much higher and is normally based on group volume)

Creating these barriers means that people who aren't salespeople simply won't sign up as distributors just to get the wholesale price, hence creating "barriers to signing up" as a distributor to the company. To get the product, they must buy it from authorized distributors, who can then make the markup between the distributor wholesale price and a reasonable retail price. This approach allows for legitimate retail markup that the distributor earns as soon as the product is sold, with no need to wait for a commission check from the company.

The big advantage of the barriers-to-entry strategy is that the retail margin is somewhat protected. Very few distributors sign up just to get the product at wholesale. Another advantage is that everyone listed on the company's computer is a salesperson, sales leader, or dream-builder. This means that the research, the marketing, and the communications strategy with the distributors is much easier.

Another advantage to this strategy is the integral part it plays in the party plan business model. Party plan companies were originally direct sales but not multi-level marketing. Many party plan companies now have multi-level commission plans, but most are still barrier-to-signup companies. The reason for this is that, as you work through the whole business model of "salesperson- hostess-attendees,", it's difficult to make the open-enrollment strategy work. Some companies have made open enrollment work, but the barriers-to-signup model tends to fit better with party-plan companies. The party-plan model is certainly a successful, effective direct sales—and now multi-level—business model, so either barriers to signup will be with us for a long time, or companies will figure out how to use open enrollment in a party plan.

Another pro to the barrier-to-signup model is that commission plans can be much simpler because a large portion of the sales commission is paid "outside the plan." To a large degree, salespeople are taken care of, regardless of how the commission plan is put together.

This takes a tremendous burden off of the designers of the commission plan.

There are disadvantages, however. One is that it forces the distributor to determine, up front, whether a potential distributor will become a salesperson or simply remain a consumer. Sometimes, sponsors err on the side of keeping people as consumers rather than as distributors. Or they can make the error the other way, and then they don't earn any sales commission. So it forces distributors to make judgments about people rather than letting the people judge themselves.

Another disadvantage to this strategy is that it's difficult to pay the product evangelists. The barriers-to-entry strategy typically does an excellent job of paying salespeople, sales leaders, and dream-builders. But In an open-enrollment strategy, it's easier to design a plan that pays the product evangelists as well.

The last disadvantage is that often the barriers-to-signup companies don't have the names and addresses of the end consumers. This can cause a problem because if a salesperson quits, all of those customers "quit" with him or her because the company doesn't know how to contact them. I've discussed this problem with executives from several large barriers-to-signup companies, and it's a frustrating problem to them. Companies are trying to create incentives to get the names of the consumers, or have the consumers order online—anything to keep from continually losing them when salespeople quit.

Barrier-to-signup has become almost the exclusive domain of party-plan companies. More and more party-plan companies have multi-level commission plans. It has been interesting to watch over the last ten years as party plans started to adopt MLM plans. Many people in the network marketing industry basically said, "See, we had the right model," but the party-plan companies retained much of their essential nature, including barriers to signup. Over the last few years, several of the companies using multi-level party plans have been the fastest-growing companies in the direct sales industry. This has caused many people to take a closer look at what they're doing right.

This scrutiny has created a new trend that has been evolving over the last few couple of years since the advent of the Internet, which is kind of a combination of open enrollment and barriers-to-signup. I call it a mini-barrier plan. In this plan, everyone signs up as a "preferred consumer" and purchases product at the preferred consumer price that is between the distributor price and the retail price. Then at some point, those who meet certain qualifications are allowed to start purchasing product at the distributor price, and they receive the retail profit of the preferred consumers they have recruited in a commission check from the company. It's an interesting combination that is only now starting to see wider use, but I think is an indication of the kind of changes that are coming to companies and commission plans as a result of the Internet. I am often asked which of these methods I think is best. I can argue the pros and cons endlessly. In some cases, when you look at the product line of a company, the method to use is very clear, and, in other cases, it seems like either method could work. In the end, it depends on the company's products, strategy, and mission.

Once a company picks a strategy, it's of critical importance that it not deceive itself. If the plan is an open-enrollment strategy, the company must not promise distributors they will earn "retail markup." If the plan is a barrier-to-signup strategy, the distributors can earn money outside the plan in the form of retail margin, and the company can count on it.

Most of all, once the strategy is in place, the company must move on and protect the strategy. So for example: if you are a barriers to signup company, don't erode the barriers to sign up. This destroys your salespeople's ability to earn commissions. If you are open enrollment, don't continually talk about retail consumer programs, unless you can create truly compelling reasons for a consumer to join a retail program instead of becoming a distributor.

I think that over the next few years each of these business models will evolve rapidly, primarily because of the rapid penetration of the Internet in our Industry. For example in June 2002, the DSA surveyed over 1800 distributors of several direct sales companies. An amazing eighty-seven percent of those distributors used the Internet in their business, compared to a sixty percent nationwide usage.

Understanding Multi-Level Commissions

Section Three: Putting Everything Together

In this last section, I'm putting together everything that I've talked about so that you can see how it all ties together. In Chapter Nine, I review the different commission plans that have been used. I give an overview of the plans, as well as the strengths and weaknesses. In Chapter Ten, I discuss how a company can create a commission earnings emphasis and which plans lend themselves to each emphasis. I also talk about which plans work well to pay sales commissions and sales management commission, and how a company can target earnings to each of the five distributor types. Then in Chapter Eleven, I review where I think commission plans are going in the new few years.

Chapter Nine

Key Topics

Overview	151
Review	153
Party plans	154
Traditional network marketing	155
Stairstep	156
Overview	156
Commission types used	156
Details	156
Strengths and Weaknesses	158
Strengths	158
Weaknesses	159
Summary	160
Unigen	160
Overview	160
Commission types used	160
Details	161
Strengths and Weaknesses	163
Strengths	163
Weaknesses	164
Summary	164
Unilevel	164
Overview	164
Commission types used	165
Details	165
Strengths and Weaknesses	167
Strengths	167
Weaknesses	167
Summary	167
Hybrid Unilevel	168

Understanding Multi-Level Commissions

- Overview 168
- Commission types used 168
- Details 168
- Strengths and Weaknesses 171
  - Strengths 171
  - Weaknesses 171
- Summary 171
- Matrix 172
  - Overview 172
  - Commission types used 172
  - Details 172
  - Strengths and Weaknesses 174
    - Strengths 174
    - Weaknesses 174
  - Summary 174
- Binary 175
  - Overview 175
  - Commission types used 175
  - Details 176
  - Strengths and weaknesses: 178
    - Strengths 178
    - Weaknesses 179
  - Summary 179
- Conclusion 180

Section Three: Putting Everything Together

What are the most common commission plans?

Overview

In this chapter, we will review the six standard multi-level commission plans and the two standard business models that use multi-level commission plans. In more than twenty years in the network marketing industry, I have seen many hundreds of commission plans, and I don't think any two have been exactly the same. However, they're all made up of a combination of:

- One or more of the standard commission types.
- A set of rules to advance from rank to rank.
- A set of rules to qualify to receive commissions.
- Typically some downline structure requirements.

Over the years, from these hundreds of wide ranging commission plans, six have come to the forefront as standard commissions plans. To be considered a standard plan, it must be used by companies over a period of several years, and its payout properties, strengths, and weaknesses need to become generally known in the industry.

A frequently asked question is, "Why are there so many different plan types that are so fundamentally and philosophically different from each other?" The reason is that commission plans have evolved from two radically different concepts.

1. Focusing on paying the salesperson first and adding the multi-level commissions to pay sales leaders later.

2. Focusing on paying the multi-level commissions first and figuring out how to handle other issues such as salesperson commissions later.

As we will see, these two design methods lead to radically different commission strategies, so it's important to understand the concepts behind each of these strategies.

Understanding Multi-Level Commissions

The ***sales commissions first*** method was spawned with the first commission plans. Companies used this strategy for two reasons. The first reason was that they were adding multi-level commissions to an existing direct sales commission plan. The second reason resulted from the technological limitations of the day. Because they did not have computers, companies simply could not deal with each and every distributor. So companies had the concept of "direct" distributors who warehoused the product and distributed it to their consumers and downline distributors. Additionally, these "direct" distributors paid the commissions due to the downline distributors directly; the company did not get involved.

In the late 1970s, the technological innovations we talked about in Chapter Two allowed companies to start dealing with all distributors, shipping the product direct from the home office and paying commissions to all distributors, taking that burden off of the direct distributors. This was the beginning of the modern network marketing industry.

Most of these companies felt that they were relieving these distributors of administrative burdens that the distributors were not very good at, and giving them more time to do the things they were good at: selling, training, and supporting their consumers.

Since all distributors were now dealing "directly" with the company, the term "breakaway" replaced the old term "direct," because when distributors went "direct" they had to "break away" from their sponsors to form their own groups. The term "breakaway" is still very confusing to people who first come into the industry.

Now that companies were dealing with all distributors, commission plans had to be modified to pay commissions to all distributors, and rules for advancement and qualifications had to be modified to make them easier for the computer to calculate. But the basic philosophy of these plans remained the same. They're built in two parts. The first part is the sales commissions, and the second part is the sales management commissions paid on the group volume of the breakaway distributor.

Over time, more of the commissions have moved from sales commissions to sales management commissions, but these plans still typically pay substantial sales commissions.

The ***multi-level commissions first*** method came along in the early 1980s, several years after the advent of the modern network marketing industry. The basic selling feature of the early versions of these plans was, "You always have more people on your sixth level than your first level, so it's a waste of money paying commissions on your first level." The reasoning continued, "If everyone sponsored only five people, a distributor would have 3,125 times as many people on her sixth level as she would on her first level."

Initially, these plans did not concern themselves with the split between sales commissions and sales management commissions. They were built on the premise that every distributor would build a large downline and therefore become a sales leader. The entire commission plan was built around that premise. Originally, these plans were built around a level commission and nothing else. Over the last twenty years, they've added other features to more effectively compensate salespeople and sales management.

Review

It's been more than twenty years since the age of the modern network marketing company began, and these two methodologies of approaching commission plan design are still the only two methods in use. The payout models of the plans themselves have started to overlap, but the starting points for designing a plan are still as different as they were twenty years ago.

The **sales commission first** strategy is still a two-part method with the sales commissions portion of the commission plan designed first and then the sales management portion of the plan designed separately. These plans are "breakaway" plans, and much about them has changed in the last twenty years, but they have stayed true to this basic concept of designing a commission plan.

The strategy of designing **multi-level commissions first** still focuses on building a backbone downline commission percentage first and then adding on any salesperson, or sales management commissions deemed necessary to fill out the plan.

Of the six standard commission plans that we will be reviewing in this book, four are multi-level first plans: unilevel, hybrid unilevel, matrix, and binary. The two sales commission first plans are stairstep and unigen.

All of these commission plans have been used enough to be defined as a standard commission plan; however, it's quite important to note that there are two very different business models that companies paying multi-level commissions use. These two business models are typically known as party plan and traditional network marketing. These two business models have very different needs when it comes to commission plans.

Party plans

Party plans cut across many lines. For a long time, traditional party plans didn't pay multi-level commissions and therefore were not considered network marketing companies. However, many party plans are becoming part of the network marketing industry. In 2001, the oldest party-plan company of all, Avon, added multi-level commissions to its commission plan.

Party-plan companies use almost every type of commission plan; however, they usually tend to use variations of the stairstep and unigen plans because of the party plan's focus on paying the salespeople. There are two key differences in how party-plan companies use commission plans and how traditional network marketing companies use the same commission plans:

1. Party-plan companies devote much more of the commissions to paying the salespeople and less to paying sales management than a traditional network marketing does.

2. Party-plan companies use the barrier-to-signup strategy, so a distributor can make retail profit in addition to commissions earned in the commission plan.

In addition to these commission plan differences, a party-plan company is a quite different company from the ground up than its traditional network-marketing cousins. Even though the commission plan itself looks much like a traditional commission plan, there are usually rules designed around the party plan dealing with such things as hostess gifts, party order gifts, and so on. As I mentioned in Chapter Five—the chapter about rules—the percentages define what a leader earns, but the character of a plan is created by the rules the company creates. So the character of a party plan is not defined as much by the percentages as it is by the rules: the barriers to signup, the qualifying volume, the party gifts, and so on.

In 1999 and 2000, many traditional network marketing companies had slow growth years. However, several party-plan companies had very successful years, I believe this was because they place more emphasis on salesperson commissions and taking care of the consumer.

Traditional networkers have said that because these companies don't pay their dream-builders enough, they have no future. However, over the last few years, some of these companies have had the most solid growth in the industry. And I find it hard to argue with success. So if I were starting a company today, I would look long and hard at, not only the commissions, but also the incentives and promotions that traditional party plans have used.

Traditional network marketing

Traditional network marketing companies use all six commission plan types. Most of these companies now adopt some form of the open enrollment strategy. Because almost everyone who buys product on a regular basis signs up as some form of a "distributor" and purchases product directly from the company, virtually all commissions earned by the distributor are paid out by the company.

These companies are built around products that are demonstrated one on one, or in very large meetings rather than in small groups of in-home demonstrations. One of the strengths of these companies is that distributors can participate in remote sponsoring. The business model was already set up for the Internet because everyone was

Understanding Multi-Level Commissions

already on the company's computer. In fact, as a result of the Internet revolution, these two business models have started to merge and cross over, to take the best ideas from each other. There's a new class of company that's starting to take the best ideas of both methods. This is the new mini-barrier company we talked about earlier.

As I discuss the six standard commission plans, I won't discuss the differences between how party plan and traditional network marketing companies use the plans. I've already covered most of these issues. This section is not intended to be an in-depth analysis of these commission plans, but simply a summary review.

Stairstep

Overview

I've never determined for certain where *stairstep* got its start. When I started in this business in 1980, stairstep was in its heyday. Forever Living and Meadow Fresh were some of the big players using stairstep. The stairstep plan has been the staple of modern network marketing companies from the late 1970s to the mid-1990s.

Commission types used

The basic stairstep commission plan uses two commission types. It uses the differential commission to pay the product evangelist and salesperson for selling the product, and it uses a level commission paid on group volume to pay the sales leader and the dream-builder for sales management. Most stairstep commission plans also have some small pool commissions or an infinity commission, but these commissions are typically a very small percentage of the overall payout.

Details

If you recall from Chapter One, the modern network marketing companies began to deal directly with all the distributors due to advances in technology. Previously, commission plans were calculated by hand and only the top sales leaders were paid by the company. These leaders then calculated what their downlines should be receiving and paid them accordingly. The stairstep evolved in this new computer age; it was designed to be calculated by the computer. It is, in fact, almost too complex to be calculated by hand. I've spent many hours recalculating a single recap.

The stairstep plan is a good match with an open enrollment strategy. The sponsor simply signs up the new distributor, and the stairstep plan provides a good automated system for allowing distributors to self-determine what type of distributor they want to be. If the distributor is a consumer, then the commission plans ensures that the sponsor always makes twenty percent on that consumer's purchases. If the distributor becomes a sales leader, the sponsor makes "generation overrides" on that person. It's all done automatically without anyone worrying about it.

These plans can then be "seasoned to taste" with commission pools, automobile funds, and other items. If you're not sure how these commissions work, the exercises in Appendix D will show you how to calculate each of these commission types.

The stairstep commission takes care of paying the product evangelists. You can configure it to provide a way for the salespeople and sales leaders to earn $500 per month relatively quickly. As noted in the earlier discussion of differential commissions, the weakness with this type of commission is that when a distributor and his sponsor both reach the top step, the sponsor never again earns any stairstep commission on that distributor. This is where the leader or generation commissions come in. At that point, the downline distributor "breaks away" and becomes a leader and becomes the sponsor's first-generation leader. As you see in Figure 19,

Understanding Multi-Level Commissions

Figure 19

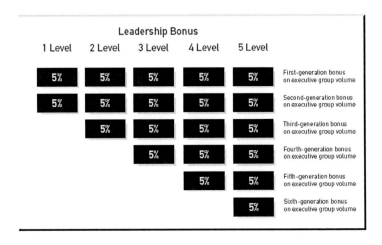

a typical generation commission is around five to six percent and paid on three to seven generations. It's very rare these days to see a company that doesn't do compression of unqualified leaders. Because leader commissions are paid on the group volume of leaders, thereby creating hubs of activity because it's more difficult to become a leader, and because compression is usually applied, the payline for generation commissions is typically much deeper than an equivalent number of levels for unilevel or hybrid unilevel plans.

Strengths and Weaknesses

Strengths

1. The plan does a great job of paying salespeople and automatically dividing the sales commission between product evangelists and salespeople.

2. The plan uses level commissions on group volume for paying sales leaders; it's the most successful method for paying sales management commissions ever found.

3. The fact that one commission type is used to pay salespeople and another is used to pay sales management simplifies design and the creation of qualifications.

4. The characteristics of the stairstep plan are well known. Companies and distributors alike know how it behaves, and so no one is surprised when the commission checks arrive.

5. A high percentage of the most successful companies are still using some form of it today.

6. It's an easy plan on which to pay a worldwide integrated seamless commission plan.

Weaknesses

1. Its characteristics are very well known. It's hard to make it sexy, exciting, and the latest new thing.

2. In the past, many front-end loading schemes hid behind the skirts of stairstep; therefore, many people associate stairstep with front-end loading. It's not fair, but then, as I tell my children, life is not fair. Many great companies have stairstep plans and don't front-end load.

3. The "breakaway is takeaway" mentality. As I explained before, in a stairstep plan, there is typically a monthly group volume requirement of between $750 and $3,000 per month. When someone you sponsor climbs to the top, at that point they break away, and from then on, neither their volume nor anyone underneath them will count toward your monthly group volume requirement. In my experience, this single issue causes the most resentment against stairstep. I certainly understand the frustration people feel about having to time and time again rebuild group volume as leaders break away. It must seem like the Greek god Sisyphus, whose punishment

was to every day roll a great stone up a mountain, only to have to do it all over again the next day.

4. The differential commission is the one whose workings distributors have the most difficulty understanding.

Summary

Stairstep has been out of favor for the last five years or so in North America. However, in Asia and Europe, it has never fallen out of favor. So we haven't seen a lot of companies start up with this type of plan; however, many successful existing plans still use it, and it's regaining popularity in North America again.

Some of the new stairstep commission plans that companies are creating have some modifications, and it will be interesting to see what happens over the next few years with the venerable old stairstep plan.

Unigen

Overview

The u*nigen* plan goes back about twenty-five years. It has roots that are much like stairstep. The single most successful company to use the unigen plan is NuSkin, although during the 1980s several other very successful companies also used the plan. Many people mistakenly call the unigen plan a stairstep plan. They're quite different, but interestingly enough, their payout model can be made to be almost the same.

Commission types used

The unigen plan, in its default configuration, uses three commission types. It uses a level commission paid on personal volume and a single level commission paid on group volume to pay the salespeople. And it uses a level commission paid on group volume to pay for sales management. Like stairstep plans, many unigen plans also have some small pool commissions or an infinity commission, but these commissions are typically a very small percentage of the overall payout.

Details

A unigen plan is built on a three-step process:

1. Create a simple plan to pay product evangelists for referrals by giving them a simple level commission for the few people they sponsor.

2. Focus on creating a solid commission for the salesperson who creates a group of product evangelists and consumers. The more consumers and product evangelists they sign up, and the more product they sell, the higher the commission they make. This is accomplished by using a variable percentage single-level commission.

3. Pay the sales leader and dream-builder for sales management using a level commission on the group volume of the salespeople.

It's a pretty straightforward concept for a commission plan. Let's walk through an example of how a unigen plan pays.

The unigen is a unilevel commission in which a distributor, Mary, makes a unilevel commission, typically down to a maximum of three levels on her downline distributors. Then at some point, a qualifier allows Mary to become a breakaway. When this happens, she typically makes a seven to fifteen percent commission on her entire group volume, which is anyone in her downline who hasn't become a breakaway or isn't under another breakaway: in other words, anyone to whom Mary is their first upline breakaway. Then when someone in her downline, John, becomes a breakaway, everyone under John is part of his group until someone in *his* downline breaks away, and so on. When someone becomes a breakaway, the generation aspects of this plan are paid just like stairstep.

Understanding Multi-Level Commissions

Figure 20

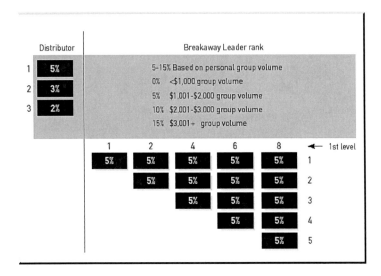

Figure 21

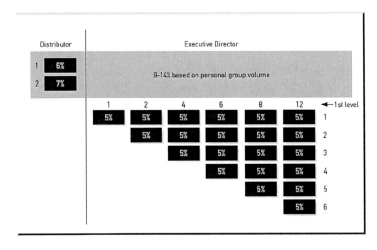

Many of the strengths and weaknesses of the unigen plan are much the same as those of the stairstep plan. You can see this in the two examples above. The first, Figure 20, is an example of the plan used by a company called Cernitin, which was very popular in the mid-1980s. The second example is similar to a plan that NuSkin uses. In a functional manner, the real difference between this plan and the stairstep plan is that the unigen plan does an excellent job of rewarding salespeople and sales leaders and does a good job of rewarding dream-builders.

It does have some strange anomalies that can catch you if you aren't watching. For example, a salesperson who qualifies for the single-level commission makes more money on first-level sales than on personal sales. This means that companies have a hard time encouraging distributors to make retail sales. The advantage is that now with the advent of the Internet, companies can encourage distributors to sign up their consumers as preferred consumers, and then pay them the first-level commission. This gives the company the added advantage of knowing who its retail consumers are.

The combination of unilevel and single-level commissions are not as good at auto-adjusting commissions between product evangelists and salespeople as the differential commission in a stairstep commission plan; however, it's much easier to understand than the stairstep, so who knows which is really best?

Like the stairstep plan, one of the real advantages of this plan is that, because you have two commission types specifically set aside for paying salespeople and one commission specifically set aside for paying sales management, it's much easier to set the percentages and qualifications to achieve the desired results. As a result, professional distributors can be better taken care of with this plan.

Strengths and Weaknesses

Strengths

1. The plan does a great job of paying salespeople; of all of the standard commission plans, this one has the strongest potential in this area.

2. The plans uses level commissions on group volume for paying sales leaders, the most successful method for paying sales management commissions.

3. The fact that it has defined certain commission types to pay salespeople and another commission type to pay sales management simplifies design and the creation of qualifications.

4. It encourages the registration of every consumer with the company, and, with the advent of the Internet, this is something many companies are looking for.

5. It's an easy plan on which to pay a worldwide integrated seamless commission plan.

6. The two commission types used are easy to understand.

Weaknesses

1. It's a breakaway plan which some distributors don't like.

2. It's not new and exciting.

3. It has not been used by enough companies that people feel comfortable with the behavior of the plan

4. It's sometimes viewed as a compromise plan.

Summary

In certain circumstances, the unigen plan has a lot to offer a company. It's reasonably simple, but can be designed to create focus on getting commissions to either salespeople or sales leaders based on the needs of the company.

Unilevel

Overview

There's a great debate among the graybeards in the network marketing industry about what the term *unilevel* means. When I first started, it meant that the commission plan had no ranks. The only commission paid was a level commission and all distributors that qualified were paid the same percentages on their downline. The example I gave in the preface of this book was a true unilevel. Other people may have different definitions how unilevel came to be, but that's how I remember it, and, after all, this is my book.

Commission types used

There are not many pure unilevels any more most of them have added the concept of ranks to receive additional levels of commissions, or higher percentages on levels, or both. But they're still called unilevel commission plans.

Unilevel plans use only one commission type, the level commission type. Since the late 1980s, most have used compression to increase payout. As a result, companies must compensate both salespeople and sales management with the level commission.

It has proven difficult to create a clear strategy for compensating salespeople and sales management with the level commission. As we talked about in Chapter Four, the level commission is not particularly well suited to creating the *entire* commission for salespeople. The second problem is that, while a level commission is well suited to sales management commissions, it works much better if it's paid on group volume rather than personal volume, and a unilevel pays everything on personal volume.

As a result of these issues, we don't see many pure unilevels anymore.

Details

The unilevel plan is built around the principle of "simple is always better." It was created as a response to the distributor burnout caused by the very high qualifications of the commission plans of the early 1980's. The original unilevel plans were models of simplicity. The only qualifications they used were a personal sales qualification, which qualified a distributor for all commissions.

Since the late 1980s, most unilevels have looked more like the modified unilevel plan in the Figure 22. That has caused the quali-

Understanding Multi-Level Commissions

fications to become more complex, but unilevels are still by far the simplest of the major commission plan types. In the example shown, it would be typical that to receive any commissions there would be a monthly personal sales requirement. Then, in order to advance from 1-Star to 2-Star, a distributor would need to have two personally sponsored 1-Stars. And in order to advance from a 2-Star to a 3-Star, a distributor would need to have four personally sponsored 1-Stars, and so on, to advance to each rank.

Unilevel plans, as the graphic shows, tend to start out paying a few levels and then add levels as the distributors build their organizations. In this example, the plan starts with five percent paid down three levels, then increases to five percent paid down four levels, and then five percent paid down five levels, and then perhaps five percent paid down six levels. In some plans, the percentage paid is increased as well as increasing the number of levels paid.

The unilevel is fine for creating middle-of-the-road commissions, but it doesn't target earnings well to specific types of distributors.

Figure 22

Pure Unilevel	Modified Unilevel Bonus Plan			
Pure Unilevel	1 Star	2 Star	3 Star	4 Star
5%	5%	5%	5%	5%
5%	5%	5%	5%	5%
5%	5%	5%	5%	5%
5%		5%	5%	5%
5%			5%	5%
5%				5%

Section Three: Putting Everything Together

Strengths and Weaknesses

Strengths

1. It spreads the wealth.
2. It's not a difficult plan, and therefore it doesn't burn people out.
3. It's easy to understand; distributors are not confused by it.

Weaknesses

1. Earnings are not targeted to salespeople or sales management.
2. Distributors aren't paid a lot to work with any one consumer. A distributor once described building an organization in a unilevel plan as "throwing mud against a wall and hoping it sticks." Unilevels are also prone to stacking because the plan doesn't target earnings well, and the requirements aren't very high. If stacking becomes rampant in a company, then volume moves out of distributors payline very quickly, lowering overall earnings even more.

Summary

The industry hasn't seen many pure unilevels over the last few years. We see quite a few of them start up, but not very many succeed. As a consequence, anything called a unilevel is almost always a unilevel hybrid, which is the next plan we talk about.

There are two places that a pure unilevel has possibilities. One is in a barrier-to-signup company where the salesperson earns the sales commission at the time of the sale in the form of retail profit. The second possibility that people talk about is in a true "referral marketing" company, like the amazon.com referral program which we will talk about a little later.

But certainly the biggest contribution the unilevel has made to the industry is the creation of the hybrid unilevel.

Hybrid Unilevel

Overview

Most of the plans that are called unilevels today are actually hybrid unilevels. They're unilevels with infinities, unilevels with fast starts, or unilevels with pools; some are in fact, "low-volume breakaways." All of these plans started out with a unilevel plan as the backbone, and then have added other commissions to pay salespeople and/or sales leaders. The difficulty in talking about this type of commission plan is that this is a very broad category indeed.

Commission types used

What all of these plans have in common is that they start out with a level commission as their primary commission. Then companies use virtually every one of the other three commission types to get more money into the hands of the salesperson for taking care of the consumer. Then a company must also deal with the issue of creating incentives for the dream-builders to keep building their organizations. These are the two major weaknesses of the traditional unilevel.

Details

The hybrid unilevel starts where the pure unilevel leaves off; the plan has added additional commission types to build on the simple appeal of the unilevel. The first hybrids appeared on the scene in the mid-1990s, and there were a couple of very notable successes.

One of these early successes was New Vision International, an open-enrollment company headquartered in Scottsdale, Arizona. They opened their doors in 1995 and signed up more than a million distributors in their first three years in business. Just a year or two later, another success story with another variation of the hybrid unilevel was Morinda, who in their first three years in business grew from zero to $30,000,000 per month in business.

Section Three: Putting Everything Together

These successes with a hybrid unilevel commission plan have insured that this commission plan would be with the industry for a long time.

One of the difficulties in talking about the hybrid is the fact that there are wide variations in the plans from company to company. In fact, if you look at the plans of the two companies I just mentioned, some people would argue that they're not the same commission plan at all! I certainly understand that argument, but when you break down commission plans into their component pieces, they're in fact the same basic type.

Hybrid unilevels typically deviate from unilevels in three areas. These differences are:

1. Hybrid unilevels tend to have more ranks and the qualifications tend to be much more difficult for the higher ranks. This is because these companies are trying to increase the earnings potential for the dream-builders, typically a problem in traditional unilevels.

2. In addition to the level commission, they tend to have other commissions or other methods to increase earnings for the sales leaders and dream-builders. Some of the common things companies do are to:

    a. Create pool commissions for the top ranks

    b. Create infinity commissions for the top ranks

    c. Actually convert from a level commission paid on personal volume to a level commission paid on group volume, which can make a tremendous difference in the amount of money earned.

    d. Implement dynamic compression

3. Hybrids create methods for increasing the earnings of the salesperson, Common methods of doing this are:

a. Fast start commissions

b. Giving salesperson rebates on all sales over a certain amount each month (for example, all purchases over $100 per month are paid under a different commission plan)

c. Creating a "mini-barrier plan" that has everyone sign up as preferred consumers and then automatically advance to distributors when they qualify (see Chapter Eight on barriers-to-signup).

d. Adding a small differential or single-level commission on the front of the plan. Typically, this is done as overlapping infinity commissions at the intermediate ranks (for example, the 3-Star thru 5-Star in a 7-Star plan)

e. Have the level commission percentages change as a distributor's ranks change.

I realize that it seems as though these techniques are all wildly different But actually, depending on the percentages used and the qualifications created for each commission, it's surprising how similar the payouts end up even using different methods.

Most hybrid unilevel plans have sales volume qualifiers to reach the higher ranks that are often as high as contemporary breakaway plans. The big difference between the hybrid unilevels and the breakaways comes from the monthly qualifiers. In breakaway plans, once distributors achieve the rank of breakaway, their sales volume no longer helps their sponsors achieve their monthly qualifications. In many hybrid unilevels, that isn't true. Sponsors achieve their monthly qualifying volume either by total organizational volume or by the volume within some number of levels. The sponsor, therefore, never has volume "breakaway" and he never has to replace that volume.

The other major difference is that percentages in the hybrid uni-levels are paid on the *personal* volumes in the downline. The generation commissions in the stairstep are paid on the *group* volumes of the downline sales leaders. This means that the generation commissions are typically much larger and the distributor is paid much deeper into his or her organization. In other words, the payline is much deeper.

Strengths and Weaknesses

Strengths

1. The hybrid retains much of the mystique and popularity of the "simple, easy to understand" original unilevel.

2. It has been used by two very successful companies, and it's not burdened down with the baggage of having been around for many years with distributors getting to know its weaknesses.

3. Because of the many variations, companies truly can create a unique commission plan for themselves.

Weaknesses

1. It starts with the unilevel commission, which is neither a sales commission nor a sales management commission. So companies have to build up both ends.

2. The behaviors of the plan are not well understood, so distributors may be expecting one thing and have another thing happen. This often requires the company to spend more time training distributors on the commission plan.

3. People expect unilevels to be simple and easy, and many hybrids are as complex and difficult as stairsteps and unigens. This can create distributor frustration.

Summary

The hybrid is the newest of the commission plans, which means that there are lots of new things to be tried and lots of innovations to be made. But as the old saying goes, "The trouble with being a pioneer sometimes is you end up dead by your wagon." If a company isn't careful with a hybrid plan, this can happen to them.

If you're thinking about starting a company using this type of a commission plan, spend the time and energy to create realistic data models with lots of variations of the plan. Run dozens of commission runs before you decide on a final commission plan so you know exactly what you have when you're finished.

As we have seen, companies who do this and can confidently tell their distributors how the plan is going to pay can have real success with this type plan.

Matrix

Overview

As I discussed earlier, a matrix plan is mainly a unilevel plan with the primary focus on the limited-width structure. Many of the early proponents of this type of plan promoted some variation on the theme of "everyone will become a sales leader." So the idea was that the structure of the plan would make it easier for everyone to attain and maintain.

Commission types used

Matrix plans originally used level commissions paid on personal volume exclusively. So it was, in fact, a traditional unilevel plan that limited the number of first levels any one distributor could sponsor. In the mid-1990s, matrix plans began to change; now, they often have a second commission paid on an enroller downline. Another change to come along was the advent of multi-center matrix plans which basically allowed distributors to have more than one position in the downline.

Details

Here is the crux of the problem: not everyone is a sales leader. But since the early versions of this plan treated everyone like a sales leader, they didn't have long-term success in the industry. As a result, these days when you see a structure plan, it's almost always combined with some other type of commission. In this plan, rather than focusing on the percentages or even on the rules, you focus on the structure.

Section Three: Putting Everything Together

Forced Matrix: The word "matrix" is a misnomer; it's really a tree structure with more than two nodes on it. A forced matrix is a structure that pays a unilevel commission, but only allows a distributor to recruit a certain number of first level distributors, typically three to five. The theory behind this type of plan is that it requires the upline to help the downline. This ensures that a few distributors don't keep all the good people for themselves.

The payout in a forced matrix is almost always a unilevel commission. A relatively new twist on the forced matrix is the enroller commission. As an "enroller," you can still get credit for the sales of your recruits beyond the three- to five-person limit, if you place additional recruits under one of your first-level people.

Figure 23

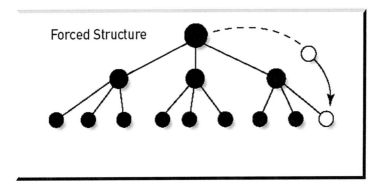

Originally, two types of forced matrixes were most common: a 3x9 structure (three first-level distributors wide and nine levels down from the recruiting distributor) and a 5x7 structure (five first-level distributors wide and seven levels deep). However, forced matrix structures have typically produced low commission checks for two main reasons. The first is the issue I talked about earlier—that no more than forty percent of the participants sponsored anyone—and the second is that stacking was rampant in the original matrixes.

This stacking mentality can cause big problems for a company. One company I know of had about 90,000 distributors. If the matrix were perfectly filled, the downline should have been about thirty levels deep, but actually had three times that many levels; over 90 levels deep!

This is a small summary of a matrix plan. If you are interested, InfoTrax maintains a white paper on matrix plans at www.infotraxsys.com.

Strengths and Weaknesses

Strengths

1. There isn't a lot of maintenance.

2. The plan is not difficult to deal with.

Weaknesses

1. Unlike unilevels, it doesn't reward one specific behavior. It tends to pay out in an arbitrary fashion.

2. The distributors can't get to any earnings level very quickly, and they spend a long time "crossing the desert" until they can reach a sustainable earnings level.

3. In the past, distributors have spent a lot of time waiting for someone else to build their business. They get in with the hope that someone in their upline will sponsor a lot of people and hence will build their organization for them.

4. Stacking is a problem, and this causes sales volume to move out of the distributor's payline very quickly.

Summary

The challenge structure-based plans must overcome is that the plan must reward the distributors for working with leaders where they find them—because, in my experience, it's impossible to predict where you're going to find leaders.

Binary

Overview

Binary got its start in the late 1980s during the heyday of stairstep plans. The initial selling feature was that it was much easier to maintain qualifications than in a stairstep, and that it was much easier to understand than the other plans of the day. What could be simpler? You simply sponsored two people and built those two legs. If those two legs generated business, you received commissions. If they generated a lot of business, you made a lot of money! A major selling point was that volume never moved out of your payline, no matter how many levels deep your genealogy went. Of course, when something sounds too good to be true, it usually is, and binary plans turned out to be more difficult than they seemed.

Commission types used

Most binary plans pay a pool commission in a weekly pay plan. Distributors have two first levels, and these two legs must each generate an amount of sales volume. If they do, the distributor get his share of the pool.

In the original binary plans, if each of the distributor's two downline legs generated $5,000, then the distributor received $1,500. That, of course, is the simple case. In reality, if the two legs generated more volume or if it took longer than a week, the plan became much more complex to understand. In some binary plans, a distributor is allowed to have multiple centers or multiple positions in the downline, so if they had seven centers, they could potentially earn seven X $1,500 each week, or $10,500 per week. (See Chapter Six for more on multiple business centers).

The binary does an excellent job of paying the mid- to high-end sales commissions and the low- to mid-range sales management commissions. This is its strength, and probably the reason it has survived these many years. It does not do well on very low-end commissions or high-end commissions, but it does very well for the mid-range commissions.

In the last five years, many binary plans have added enroller downlines that are not limited in width and have started paying other commissions in addition to the binary commissions. Sometimes these plans split the commission between binary and enroller commissions. And sometimes these plans pay binary commissions on some products and enroller commissions on other products.

Details

When the binary commission plan first came onto the scene, it took the world by storm. It promised to really shake things up, and it did. For those of us in the network marketing software business, it took us several years before we really understood how binary really behaved. This is because binary brought with it so many innovations.

It's almost impossible to describe how much binary shocked the industry with its seeming simplicity and its underlying complexity. The challenge binary presented resulted from its completely opposite approach to thinking about commissions. Every other commission plan to that point was built on the following two premises:

1. Commissions are paid on a *limited* number of levels of a distributor's downline, but on an *unlimited* amount of sales volume.

2. All commissions for a given product order are paid in a single commission run

In contrast, the binary plan is built on the following two opposite premises:

1. Commissions are paid on a *unlimited* number of levels of a distributor's downline, but on a *limited* amount of sales volume.

2. Commissions for a given product order can be paid across several commission runs, and, in fact, it's impossible to know when all the commissions on a single order have been paid.

As you can see, that the basic idea was as different from previous plans as night and day, and it took a while for the distributors, the companies, and the computer programmers to all agree on what it all meant.

When I saw my first binary, our client, which was just converting to binary, told me they thought the maximum payout would be about forty-five percent. Unfortunately, they didn't realize that commissions were not all paid in one week. When we figured out what their payout would actually be, we calculated it at 115 percent, or they could pay $1.15 in commissions for every $1.00 in sales. The distributors liked that, but the company wasn't too happy. This was the kind of "voyage of discovery" that almost all of the first binary companies took until the plan was generally understood by the industry.

These are the basic concepts that a binary plan is built around:

1. A distributor sponsors two people, creating two downline "legs," and then builds a downline under those two legs.

2. Most original binaries allow distributors to have multiple centers—usually one, three, or seven centers.

3. Binaries pay their downline commissions once a week.

4. Distributors have to generate downline sales volume that is "balanced" between the two downline legs. When they reach certain levels of sales volume, they receive a commission check. They can accumulate sales volume in one week or across several weeks.

5. Original binary companies had the computer place automatically distributors in the downline, a method that created some real problems. For example, if you have two very strong recruiters and they both end up in the same downline leg, instead of one in each, if the mistake isn't caught

immediately, there's no way to fix it. This is because other distributors have been placed under those people, and so on. This can be disastrous for a distributor.

To date, binaries have been sort of a mixed bag. Among certain distributor groups, binary is the only commission plan they will have anything to do with. Most distributors I know, either love them or hate them; no one I know of seems to be on the fence. Of the dozens of companies that started with binaries in the early 1990s, the only two I know of that have been truly successful for a long period of time are Usana and Market America. Both of them seem to have become very successful by taking advantage of the fact that binary inherently rewards salespeople and sales leaders better than almost any other type of plan and is weaker in rewarding the product evangelist and dream-builder. Both of these companies have built their entire recruiting strategy around this fact.

But over the last few years, we've been seeing a new crop of companies that are also finding success with the binary commission plan, using it in combination with other commission plans. So the binary plan seems to be coming of age.

If you want to understand the binary commission plan better, InfoTrax offers a detailed white paper about the plan, free for downloading at www.infotraxsys.com.

Strengths and weaknesses:

Strengths

1. Binary does an excellent job of paying the mid- to high-end sales commissions.

2. Binary also does a good job in paying the low- to mid-range sales management commissions.

3. There is a committed core of distributors who know and love the binary commission plan.

4. Its behavior is now very well understood.

Weaknesses

1. Many of the original binaries were built by promising distributors that their upline would build their downline. This created a welfare mentality.

2. Most binaries have a maximum upper limit on earnings; some distributors don't realize this.

3. Placement can be a real problem. If a distributor has only two good downline distributors, and they both mistakenly end up in one leg, it can ruin her business.

Summary

Now that binary plans have been around for ten years, we're starting to see some changes to the basic model that have solved some of the problems of the past.

Some of these new features are:

1. Distributors no longer have to evenly balance the volume on the two legs; a popular variation allows the volume to be split 1/3 – 2/3.

2. Companies are combining binary with other commission types to fix the capped earnings problem.

3. All distributors sign up via the Internet, and their sponsors place them. The company can't make mistakes in placement. Most companies have abandoned having the computer place downline distributors.

The major problem with binaries was promise of "your upline builds your downline." It seems that more and more, the new companies using binary have moved away from that, and now focus on what the binary does well: pay the salesperson and the sales leader if the distributor builds an organization.

Now that there is a core of distributors out there that understands how the binary works, companies can take advantage of its strengths and put in place measures to mitigate its weaknesses.

Conclusion

The last half of the 1990s was sort of like San Francisco in the 1960s; it was a period of experimentation. But this time it was experimentation in commission plans, not illegal chemistry. Many of these plans defy categorization; in addition to the hybrid unilevels we have talked about, there have been a lot of plans that are just plain interesting. Fast start commissions have come on strong, we seem to see infinity commissions everywhere, and we see a few so-called "double breakaways." But none of these plans has emerged from this period as a defined plan type like the ones we have reviewed in this chapter.

So where are the plans of the future taking us? That's the $64,000 dollar question, or, for our worldwide readers, the 80,000 euro question. I don't think anyone knows right now. It's clear to most of us in the industry that the network marketing industry is on course for tremendous growth. Rather than hurting the industry, as so many thought it would, the Internet is helping it. The Internet is helping to lower companies' cost of operations and to help leaders manage their groups by giving them better and timelier information about their downline. The Internet also gives distributors tools like WebMeeting, e-mail, personal web pages, and electronic newsletters for motivating, educating, training, and supporting their downline. We will talk about these issues in the last chapter.

As the work that the leaders do evolves, then the commission plans that pay them may need to evolve. I know you're thinking that early in the book I said, "Don't change a plan," but here I refer to tweaking and evolving a plan rather than making wholesale changes. What changes? I think it's too early to know exactly how to make changes, or to understand all of the ramifications of those changes—but as always, those companies that figure out the answers first will reap some great rewards.

As you think about commission plan types, don't get too caught up in the rhetoric about which commission plan is the best; for example, stairstep is the only one, or unilevel is the only plan that works. As I pointed out in Chapter Four, there are only four types of commissions: level, differential, single-level, and pool commissions. Every commission plan is made up of those four commission types. So, in some ways, there isn't an intrinsically huge difference between most of the plans. Most major types of commission plans have worked in certain situations, and all have failed in other situations. If you're thinking about joining a company or starting one, when you look at the commission plan, you should look at each commission type individually and ask yourself, "What is that specific commission going to do for me and my downline as we build our business?" If you don't know the answer to that, you need an explanation—or perhaps the plan needs some rethinking.

On the Soapbox

People ask me what plan I like best. Okay, I'll admit it. I don't like matrix plans. I never have. I like binary plans because they pay well, but the way I feel about binary plans is like the old joke. "How do you define mixed emotions? Your mother-in-law driving off a cliff in your new Cadillac." The binary plan pays well, but the structure aspects of the plan can be hard to deal with.

Stairstep plans, unigens, and other multi-part plans are the easiest to fine tune to fit with a company's strategy. I have seen a lot of companies that coordinate their commission plan with their strategy and a lot that haven't. In the end, the best plan is a plan that matches a company's mission and product line.

Understanding Multi-Level Commissions

Chapter Ten

Key Topics

Overview 185
Creating a commission plan earnings emphasis 185
Sales management commissions. 197

Understanding Multi-Level Commissions

What are commission plans designed to accomplish?

Overview

By now, if you're like most people, you just want to know what plan works the best, or you just want to tell me which plan works the best. Of course, the problem is that there are successful companies with each commission plan type.

In the last chapter, we discussed the different commission plans. In this chapter, I want to talk about what they can and should be designed to accomplish. I will talk first about creating an earnings emphasis in a plan. Then we'll finish up with which plans work and don't work for paying sales commissions and sales management commissions, as well as each of the distributor types that make up those two categories.

On the Soapbox

Economic Equation

Consider this equation: If you are only considering the economic factors, when a distributor adds up all the time it takes to find and service customers and distributors, then divides those hours by the money he can reasonably expect to receive for those efforts, the result is a "per hour" price for his time. If this amount is less than what he could earn flipping burgers at a fast-food place, that distributor will ultimately leave the company. You must keep this cold, hard fact before you from the very beginning of your commission plan design.

Creating a commission plan earnings emphasis

Simply stated, commission plan earnings emphasis occurs when a commission plan allows one or more types of distributor to make a higher percentage of commissions on some or all of their downline sales volume than other types of distributors

Understanding Multi-Level Commissions

Lets consider a simple case of commission plan emphasis. A fairly typical commission plan these days pays five percent on downline volume; however, by adding additional commission types, it's possible for a company to allows some types of distributors to earn fifteen percent on their downline volume. What difference would commission emphasis make in this case? For simplicity, we'll assume that each person in their downline purchased $100.00 of product.

Figure 24

Number of Distributors	Tatal Downline Sales Volume	Emphasized Earnings (15% Commission)	Non-Emphasized Earnings (5% Commission)
33	$3,333	$500	$166
100	$10,000	$1,500	$500
3,000	$300,000	$50,000	$15,000

1. A distributor making $500 a month will have about 33 consumers to take care of.

2. A distributor making $1,500 a month will have 100 consumers to take care of.

3. A distributor earning $50,000 a month will have a minimum of 3,000 consumers/distributors to take care of.

Which of these commission emphasis strategies is best? If depends on what a company is trying to accomplish. If a company is looking to creating incentives for working with consumers then in the case of #1 and #2, the distributor can probably give personal attention where needed; there are not too many consumers. But in the third example, it's hard to imagine that a distributor could give personal attention to 3,000 consumers. That's giving incentive for an impossible task. . If the fifteen percent emphasis was designed to reward something else—a task more appropriate to a sales leader or dreambuilder—then would be an appropriate emphasis.

Section Three: Putting Everything Together

This is the fundamental question that the management of every company must come to terms with. What level of earnings do you want to pay your distributors each month? When I am working with a group of executives who are designing a commission plan, I often have them work through the following exercise.

Suppose you have $1,000,000 available per month for paying your distributors. When you distribute that money, do you want to pay two people $500,000 each? Do you want to pay twenty people $50,000 each? Do you want to pay two thousand people $500 each? Do you want to pay twenty thousand people $50 each?

When we're designing the commission plan, I have them fill out this chart individually so we have a point of reference as to what each of them believes. If you're thinking about starting a company, stop and take some time to fill out the chart. Remember, you have a total of $1 million to pay. (Don't worry, I'll wait)

Figure 25

Amount of commission check	Number of checks	that amount
$50.00	X_____	=_____
$500.00	X_____	=_____
$1,000.00	X_____	=_____
$5,000.00	X_____	=_____
$50,000.00	X_____	=_____
$500,000.00	X_____	=_____
		=$1,000,000

If you're like most people, you created an emphasis of a certain earnings size when you filled out this chart. In other words, you created a few of most sizes of checks, but allocated a disproportionate amount of money on either small, mid-range, or large commission checks. This is the way most commission plans work; they have what I call earnings emphasis.

Commission plan earnings emphasis typically falls into one of three categories:

1. Low-end or "pay for your product" emphasis: Some commission plans allow the product evangelist to quickly earn $50-$100 per month. The reason companies do this is based on the theory that people who love a product are the greatest advertisers. So if they can get product for free, they are even greater advertisers. Many of these product evangelists may also go on to be salespeople, sales leaders, and even dream-builders.

2. Mid-range or "improve my life money" emphasis: This is the idea of getting distributors to a stable income in the range of $500 - $5,000 per month as quickly as possible. It isn't enough money to get rich, and usually isn't enough to cause someone to quit a full-time job, but it's enough to let them buy the car they want, or take a dream vacation. This amount of money changes a distributor's life enough to prompt him or her to make a genuine commitment to the company. These companies tend to enjoy an incredible degree of loyalty from their salespeople and sales leaders.

3. High-end or "making it big" emphasis: What's the definition of "making it big"? It's making "a lot more money" than the average income of the type of distributor a company is trying to attract. If a company is trying to attract doctors and lawyers, this amount has to be much higher than if it wants to attract blue-collar workers or college students. However, most of these plans emphasize commission sizes of at least $20,000 per month and up. Companies with this type of emphasis believe leadership comes from the top down, and that, in the end, everyone is reaching for the big dream.

So which is better? Although there are more successful companies that have made the mid-range strategy work, companies have been successful using all three methods.

Section Three: Putting Everything Together

No matter which emphasis a company chooses, I can tell you two things that won't work:

1. Not knowing what the emphasis of the plan is.

2. Drifting between emphases in the marketing, incentive, and commission strategies.

I know it sounds odd, but I've worked with companies that simply copied their commission plan from another company and did not know what the emphasis was. Often, they then compounded the mistake by having a product strategy and a marketing strategy that didn't match the commission emphasis of the plan they ended up with, and chaos reigned. It's like using the saying "an apple a day keeps the doctor away" to sell oranges.

Okay, enough philosophy. Let's walk through a simple example of how to create earnings emphasis.

First let's start with a commission plan that has no earnings emphasis. In a plan like this, all distributors in the company earn the same percentage on their downline sales volume regardless of their downline's size. Let's use the example of five percent. If a distributor has $1,000 in downline volume, he earns $50. If he has $10,000 in volume, he earns $500, and so on. When you graph this earnings line, it's a straight incline.

Then a company may choose one of the three areas to emphasize; this choice inevitably takes money away from the other two areas. For example, to emphasize mid-range checks, a company could reduce commission in the low end or the high end. The first option is to reduce the low-end check in some manner. You can see in Figure 26 that when a distributor reached a certain rank or group volume requirement—for example, $1,000 in group volume—he or she would get an increased percentage. Thus the "bump" up in the graph. Now the distributor is making more in the mid-range.

Figure 26

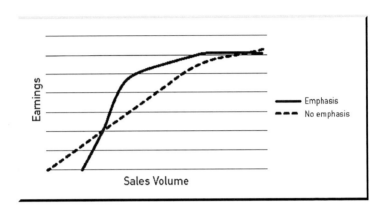

The second way would be to "use" money from the high-end checks. In Figure 27, the emphasized curve follows the straight five percent line, then jumps up again in the middle. However, this time, the line flattens out as the distributor's sales volume moves higher; eventually, earnings cap out. This shows that a straight five percent commission would give them higher earnings at the top, but it emphasizes the mid-range commissions instead.

Figure 27

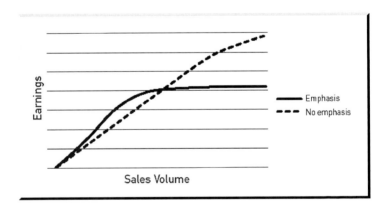

On the Soapbox

Three goals of a commission plan

In addition to keeping the revenue stream flowing so it will be profitable, a company has to consider the hopes and dreams of its distributors. As you saw in Chapter One, distributors stay with a network marketing organization only as long as it either helps them achieve their goals, or as long as they believe it will do so at some point. So, in addition to encouraging this balance between sales and recruiting, a company must itself maintain a delicate balance. A commission plan must carry much of the burden for meeting three important goals:

1. *It's important to generate enthusiasm among your distributors.* They need to consider the opportunity a company offers to be attractive. They need to believe in the product, they need to have a feeling of belonging to the team, they need to feel that they're doing something worthwhile, and they need to believe that the company will enable them to meet their financial goals. If they get to the point that they feel they're simply going through the motions, they won't meet their sales goals, because they just don't care.

2. *It's important to encourage distributors to both sell and recruit.* The company needs to encourage distributors to spend time doing what it needs them to do so the company can meet its goals as well. It needs to teach them to maintain the balance that we just talked about.

3. *It's important to retain distributors.* We all know that one of the great problems facing network marketing companies is attrition. One reason is that people get tired of the effort required to build an organization or to meet sales quotas. Another challenge is that a lot of people join companies for reasons that don't lead to success: to buy a few products for themselves at a discount, for example, or to get a pesky brother-in-law to leave them alone. The longer a company can retain the willing and competent distributors, however, the more stability that company will have. That's where the earnings come in; when distributors are seeing the money they were hoping for, they'll stick with it.

Understanding Multi-Level Commissions

Now don't get me wrong; I want to be very clear on this. Most network marketing companies still create small, mid-sized, and large commission checks. In fact, for most companies, no matter which commission plan they use and somewhat regardless of their earnings emphasis, much of their commission money is still distributed between all commission check sizes. In other words, emphasis does not eliminate the other two areas; it simply changes the number of each size of commission checks.

Some people say that any commission plan type can be adjusted to create any of the three earnings emphases; however, it has been my experience that each plan type is suitable to certain types of earnings emphasis. Here is a chart of the plan types we reviewed in the previous chapter and their traditional earnings emphasis:

Figure 28

Commission Plan type	Low	Mid-Range	High	No Emphasis
Unilevel				Yes
Hybrid Unilevel	Yes	Yes		
Stairstep	Yes	Yes	Yes	
Unigen	Yes	Yes	Yes	
Binary		Yes		
Matrix				Yes

Why are some plans able to create certain earnings emphasis and other plans are not? In order to create an earnings emphasis, a plan must have a method of increasing the commission percentages paid to distributors who have built the size of downline organization and generated the amount of sales volume that the company wants to emphasize. The way a company does this is to have multiple commission types in a commission plan: that is, one or more level commissions that create stability and long-term growth, as well as one or more other targeted types of commissions. So let's review the chart.

Unilevels and matrix plans use only level commissions in their plans. A level commission is the least targeted of all of four types of commissions, which is why those plans don't generate an emphasis. Stairstep and unigen are both based on a combination of level commissions to spread the wealth and differential or single-level commissions, which are both targeted commissions. Because they include these targeted commissions, they're able to create whatever emphasis a company wants.

A traditional binary plan is the one emphasized plan that uses a single commission type, but it's typically a type of pool commission. If you remember, pool commissions are one of the most targeted commission types, which is why a binary plan ends up being an emphasized plans toward the mid-range commission checks.

Once a company decides what emphasis, if any, it wants to use, then it can narrow the choices on which commission plan types to use. Or the company may decide to build one of the new à–la-carte plans. After the company has a general idea about the commission plan type it wants to use, the next step is to decide on specific commission strategies to provide adequate compensation for two activities: product sales and sales management. Let's review these commission plans and see how each of them deals with these two very different activities.

Commissions for Sales. Commissions for the salespeople require commission types that can be targeted to the few people who are involved in the sales process. The level commission has not been successful for sales commissions, unless used in conjunction with other commission types, because it's not a targeted commission. The plans that use only level commissions are unilevel and matrix. As a result, these plans typically have a very difficult time rewarding salespeople, *unless, and this is very important,* it's a barrier-to-signup company. In a barrier-to-signup company, the majority of the sales commission is received directly by the distributor in the form of retail profit at the time the product is sold.

In Chapter Four, we talked about the fact that differential, pool, and single-level commissions are targeted commissions. The commission plans that use these three targeted commission types to reward the salesperson are stairstep, unigen, binary, and some forms of hybrid unilevel.

Within the broad area of sales commissions, a company must still pay the individual distributor types. The three distributor types that would be affected by sales commissions are the consumer, the product evangelist, and the salesperson. Let's briefly review how commission plans affect these individual distributor types.

The consumer: For most companies, the plan for consumers falls into two parts. The first is to encourage them to become product evangelists without annoying them, and the second is to occasionally offer them opportunities to try new products. This second part is very traditional marketing. Some examples of this are free shipping for the month of April or "buy one, get one free." Another approach that's growing in popularity is a one-time referral commission or a free product for referring other consumers.

With an open-enrollment company, the consumer can become a big issue if someone signs up as a distributor, but then turns out to be a consumer. Most companies don't pay ongoing commissions, which, in most cases, are really rebates on the personal purchases of consumers. If a company decides to pay the consumer, two commission types that easily lend themselves to compensating the consumer are the differential and level commissions.

Why would a company design its commission plan to pay a consumer? Here are the pros and cons. Companies build a commission plan that pays consumers with the belief that it will encourage the consumer to move up to being a product evangelist, or even higher. The reason most don't implement this strategy is a very high financial price. As I mentioned earlier, up to seventy percent of all distributors in any open-enrollment organization never sponsor anyone. If a company has a total payout of forty percent, but gives ten percent commission to the consumer, then the company has significantly reduced the amount available to pay all other distributors. Think about it: the product evangelist found that consumer, and the salesperson, sales leader, and dream-builder serviced him or her, and now the company is limiting their earnings to thirty percent. Since almost no company emphasizes consumer rebates, this is a large amount of money to take away from the area they *are* emphasizing.

The product evangelist: A product evangelist does his work as much because of how he feels about the product and the company as he does for the money he makes. The best way to describe the compensation given to a product evangelist is a big "thank you." Traditional non-cash incentives and contests have been very successful. For example, a pool commission tied to a multi-month contest works very well. It's important to remember that by definition, product evangelists love to talk about the product, but don't want the commitment of taking care of consumer needs and problems. So the company needs to say "thank you" to them, but not saddle them with the responsibility of consumer support. As a result, the commission plan can't give them all the sales commission, because then no one would be paid to take care of the consumer.

The product evangelist is important to a company's success because there are potentially so many of them. If a company has a great product and a good commission and incentive program, ultimately a high percentage of its distributors will be product evangelists.

Let's take a look at the compensation strategies that have been used over the years for product evangelists. Level commissions in conjunction with another commission type, or a well-designed differential commission, can both work to give the product evangelists commissions on the consumers they bring into the business. Both commission types have their pros and cons. Differential commissions can be designed to pay the product evangelist better on his or her consumers, but level commissions are much easier to understand. Another benefit of the level commission is that, in that rare instance where the product evangelist sponsors a salesperson or higher, using the differential commission, the product evangelist makes no money on that distributor, whereas with a level commission the product evangelist usually earns some money.

The salesperson: The salespeople are where the rubber meets the road. A company must have people selling product, explaining how that product works, answering the consumers' questions, holding parties, and taking care of the problems. The other major responsibility of salespeople in most companies is to recruit and support product evangelists. Product evangelist find consumers, but don't service them; the salesperson does. So the salesperson needs to be compensated to do this. If the plan doesn't adequately reward distributors for these activities, they won't do it. This lack of activity begets what I call a "hollow plan"—lots of distributors, but no sales.

As we discussed earlier, there are two ways to compensate the salespeople:

1. Pay them inside the plan.

2. Create barriers to signup, so they can be assured of actually selling product at a retail profit.

Of utmost importance, for companies and distributors alike, is figuring out how long it will take to find consumers, train them, answer product questions, and solve their problems. The plan must compensate salespeople for this time; they will figure out whether they're earning enough sales commission to make selling your product worth their time. If the answer is no, they won't spend the time making sure that consumers needs are taken care of. If that happens, the company has to take over the role, or it simply won't get done.

Salespeople make around $500 to a few thousand dollars a month. Even though they may consider this a part-time income and often have full-time jobs, if you ask them what they do, they often identify themselves as distributors of the companies for whom they sell.

The amount of commission a salesperson can earn from a commission plan depends on three factors in addition to the commission plan type. These factors are:

1. **Is the company an open-enrollment or barrier-to-signup company?** I discuss this concept at length in Chapter 8, but in summary, if the company is a barriers-to-signup company, then the salesperson can also expect to make retail profit over and above the defined plan. In an open-enrollment company, the retail profit opportunities are limited.

2. **What are the percentages paid on the "salesperson side" of the plan?** This is pretty obvious. The higher the percentages, the more a salesperson is going to make.

3. **What are the qualifications to advance in rank and receive monthly commissions?** This issue is more complex than most people think. Companies often think that the easier they make it to achieve higher ranks, the better, but this is not necessarily true. The way most commission plans determine how to pay a salesperson is that the salesperson has a higher rank in the commission plan than his or her consumers. If the company makes it so easy to achieve higher ranks that actual consumers achieve the higher ranks, then the company has effectively taken away the salesperson's commission, and no one is being paid to service the consumer. This is a bad thing.

Sales management commissions.

You don't have to study commission plans very long to realize that the backbone of sales management commissions is a level commission based on some form of group volume. This is true of unigen, stairstep, and almost all barriers-to-signup companies. Unilevel, hybrid unilevel, and matrix plans use level commissions, but they're based on personal volume, not on group volume. The only standard plan in existence that does not use a level commission to pay sales management is binary. It pays both salespeople and sales leaders using a pool commission.

Why do so many plans use the level commission type to pay the sales management? The reason is pretty clear. The level commission is the one commission type that has the ability to spread out earnings among a group of distributors. So it has both the ability to reward improving performance and the ability to create stable earnings, both of which are critical to sales leaders.

Assuming that the company is using level commissions on group volume, the amount a sales leader earns is a function of three things:

1. **What are the percentages paid and how many levels are they paid on?** This is the most obvious concern, but it

actually makes the least difference of the three. I know this doesn't seem right, but look at the following example. If one distributor earns five percent down five levels on personal volume with no compression and no group volume requirement, and another distributor earns five percent down five levels on group volume with standard compression with a group volume of $2,000 per month, the second distributor could easily make ten times as much commission as the first distributor.

2. **What type of compression does the plan use?** Compression allows sales leaders to be paid deeper on their organization—much deeper in some cases.

3. **What is the group volume requirement?** As I mentioned above, this issue probably has more effect on how much sales leaders earn than the other two issues. This is because it allows the sales leader to be paid down a number of generations on "hubs of activity."

The pool commission is also used quite often to create final enhancements to sales management commissions because of its ability to reward any specific targeted activity. For example, these commissions are often used at the very top ranks to create incentives for leaders to continue to build their organizations even after they reach the top rank. Also if, when the commission plan is modeled, there are "flat" spots in the plan, a pool commission can help alleviate them.

So, if the question of earnings for selling product and managing salespeople comes down to issues like compression, rank, and monthly qualifications, how do companies decide what is appropriate for them? That can be a painful process, and some issues, like monthly personal and group qualifications, should logically be decided after a careful consideration of the company's product line. I discussed this concept at length in Chapter Five.

The last thing we need to talk about when discussing sales management commissions is how a company can pay the individual distributor types of sales leaders and dream-builders.

Section Three: Putting Everything Together

The sales leader. One complaint I hear today is that distributors are not loyal. I think sales leaders are extremely loyal, sometimes even loyal to a fault. These are the distributors who keep a company alive. If you want to check on the health of a company, look at the income stability of the salespeople and sales leaders. I've never seen a company with a solid, stable group of salespeople and sales leaders that was not itself stable.

The sales leaders hold the meetings, lead the conference calls, put together the training, and deal with the concerns of the salespeople. They are the primary motivators of the downline. These are the distributors who keep the momentum of a company alive. All four types of commissions are used in targeting earnings to sales leaders. In the case of a stairstep, it uses differential and level commissions to compensate them. Some companies also create "qualified sales leader" pool commissions to further emphasize mid-range earnings. When companies base their commission plans around a level commission, they can use a single-level group volume commission to emphasize mid-range earnings. Unigen plans are based on this concept.

In addition to the level commission to compensate sales leaders, companies have successfully used the miscellaneous types of commissions to create incentives as distributors make their transition from salesperson to sales leader. The other kinds of incentives that are common for sales leaders are car programs or other incentives to pay for trips to conventions.

> *If you want to check on the health of a company, look at the income stability of the salespeople and sales leaders. I've never seen a company with a solid, stable group of salespeople and sales leaders that was not itself stable.*

The dream-builder: Dream-builders play an enormously important role in the company. They provide the enthusiasm and create most of the training. They provide marketing expertise and material for the various niche markets in which the company sells.

> **The commission plan design rule**
>
> A well-designed commission plan pays a decreasing percentage of increasing volume in such a way that the percentage decreases slowly enough and in small enough increments that the overall earnings always go up, never down!

Level commissions based on group sales have been the mainstay of compensating dream-builders for thirty years. Since the late 1980s, compression has been the norm. The challenge companies have to deal with in compensating dream-builders when using only the level commissions is that sooner or later sales volume starts moving out of the dream-builder's payline. Companies use four methods to deal with this issue:

1. Create an "infinity" commission added at the highest rank to provide a strong incentive to achieve it. This combination works so well because it spreads the money out among several dream-builders and allows them to be paid many levels deep on their downline.

2. Create a prorated pool commission which distributors at the top rank share

3. Continue to add more levels to the plan either by raising the payout or by cutting the payout of the mid-range distributors. (Don't laugh! I once watched a company cut all the mid-range distributors' earnings by thirty percent to give the dream-builders an extra level of payout. It wasn't pretty to watch the results).

4. Don't do anything. Many of the very successful companies today have plans that ultimately have an end to the dream-builder's payline.

As you can see, it's important that a company know what its strategy is going to be before distributors get to that point, and not drift between strategies. The bottom line is that a successful network marketing company necessitates a strong and flexible compensation plan, a plan that pays and generates activity at every level of the company. For this reason, it's important for corporate executives to build a plan that rewards their distributors—and it's important for distributors to find these types of companies.

Understanding Multi-Level Commissions

Chapter Eleven

Key Topics

Conclusion...210

Understanding Multi-Level Commissions

What is the future of commission plans?

Starting in the late 1990s, the Internet started to have a dramatic effect on how network marketing companies did business. It was a time very much like the early 1980s, when the modern network marketing industry was created. Not that the fundamental business of one person selling product to another person changed, but instead, the tools available to a company for dealing with its distributors and customers dramatically changed because of technological innovation.

In Chapter One, I talked about the fact that in the late 1970s five technologies—fast, inexpensive computers, video and audio tapes, rapid package shipment, inexpensive long distance/toll free calling, and conference calling—allowed network marketing companies to begin the transition of dealing directly with every distributor. This changed the operations of companies to their very core, and these changes brought about the modern network marketing industry. It's interesting that every multi-level commission plan in use today came into existence in the ten years following this technological revolution. These new commission plans were a response to new requirements created by the changes in the network marketing industry.

So how do these facts relate to a discussion about the future of commission plans?

I believe that the Internet is in the process of causing just as dramatic a change in the way network marketing companies operate as those that happened in the late 1970s and early 1980s. And as these changes begin to take hold, commission plans will once again go through a period of evolution. It's important that the industry manage these changes better than we did the last time around. In many ways, some of the new commission plans were designed and tested like airplanes in the early 1900s, built in garages and taken out and flown. If they flew, fine; if they crashed, build another one and find anther pilot.

Why are we at this point now if the Internet has been around for years? I mentioned several times in the book that eighty-seven percent of distributors now use the Internet in their business. This opens a huge door for network marketing companies because they can

Understanding Multi-Level Commissions

now deal not only with their distributors over the Internet, but with customers as well. In some respects, companies may soon be able to require their leaders to have access to the Internet in order to transact certain types of business with the company. Some already have.

To understand how a network marketing company can best use the Internet to fulfill its overall corporate mission, you must look back at what traditionally makes a network marketing company successful, and then see how the Internet can help a company do those things better.

One of the pioneers of modern direct sales was the Hoover Vacuum Company. Why did they sell via direct sales rather than through the established retail channel? Unless a housewife saw a demonstration of the vacuum cleaner, she would never believe that a vacuum cleaner could clean her floors and rugs better than sweeping or beating them. It certainly wouldn't be worth the money she spent. Product demonstration was the way to sell that product. They were simply going to have to prove the product worked, one housewife at a time.

Times have not changed. Today it seems there are two basic methods companies use to sell products. One is by lowering the cost of getting the product in the hands of the customer, also known as lowering physical distribution costs. The second is by improving the quality and effectiveness of motivating, educating, training, and supporting the customer, known as the intellectual distribution model. Sam Walton revolutionized the first method when he founded Wal-Mart. He threw down the gauntlet and relentlessly drove down the cost of getting product into the hands of the customer. From that day forward, it seemed every store had to decide whether to compete on price or compete on service. There was no longer a middle ground.

The concept of the discount superstore has been wildly successful at lowering the cost of everyday items. However, this success has left a tremendous opportunity for companies to sell products that require intellectual distribution, because if a product does not require some form of intellectual distribution, it will eventually be sold by the "Wal-Marts" of the world. Since these superstores are never going to sell products that require intellectual distribution, this becomes our industry's "ace in the hole".

So what does all this mean? Helping network marketing companies to sell products that require more intellectual distribution or doing a better job of intellectual distribution of the products they currently sell is the greatest untapped potential of the Internet today.

Web tools like web conferencing, online learning libraries, and downloadable documents can help the distributors understand and teach their customers about product. A company can make best use of their top motivators, best trainers, and best educators to inform and educate. Internet services can mean distributors no longer have to wait until they feel comfortable with the entire presentation before talking about product.

Why is the Internet uniquely suited to this task? Because it allows each distributor or customer to view customized information, based on their own unique needs and on a very cost-efficient basis. There has never been anything like the Internet for doing this task. A company can create hundreds of presentations, product sheets, and other means of conveying product information, and design their Internet site to show a distributor only those items they're interested in, based on what they've ordered, a survey they've filled out, or many other criteria.

The great competitive advantage the direct sales industry has always had is intellectual distribution. And, as an industry, we pay a tremendous amount in sales commissions for that advantage. So just like Sam Walton, who was relentless in improving his competitive advantage by perfecting the physical distribution model, we as an industry must be relentless in improving the intellectual distribution model. And now, for the first time in history, the Internet gives us the almost perfect tool to do it.

Why do I think this will cause the industry to go through a round of changes in commission plans? It's really quite simple when you think about it:

Understanding Multi-Level Commissions

- Commission plans reward distributor activities.
- When companies ask distributor to engage in different activities, the company must reward them for those new tasks.

This may seem like a contradiction, because I've said several times that the basic structure of a plan should not change. Both statements are true. If a company's plan encourages sales leaders and dream-builders to build their downline organizations in a certain way, there is no reason to change how the downline structure is rewarded, because the distributors cannot change their downline organization structure. But there are many changes that *can* be accommodated without destroying the value of a downline organization. It's a balancing act, to be sure; however, if you look back in the 1980s, many "direct distributor" companies did not change because they didn't want to hurt their distributors, and the changing tide of the industry washed over them. Most of the big companies survived and ultimately adapted, but some of the smaller ones did not survive. And going out of business really did hurt their distributors. A company needs that important balance between having enough consistency in its commission plan to create stability and taking advantage of improvements as they come along.

As I said, commission plans must reward distributor activities. In the past, certain distributor types performed certain functions such as training, motivation, and so on. Those distributors were compensated through the commission plan for performing these activities. Now, because of the Internet, the distribution of tasks is shifting. For example, if a salesperson previously did all the training because she lived locally, now with the Internet, web conferencing, and other means, the person best qualified may perform training functions. The commission plans must therefore evolve to pay this new person to perform the work he or she has now taken on.

So if the commission plan needs to change to pay distributors for the new activities they're performing, how does a company make the changes in their plan without "crashing the plane?" In other words, how do you take a plan currently being used and change it without destroying it?

Section Three: Putting Everything Together

This question used to be almost impossible to answer; however, two things have made it a little easier: experience and testing.

In the early 80s, everyone had experience with one type of plan. Now, those of us who have been in the industry have become familiar with many different plans using all the commission types. Understanding how each commission type works, helps us to anticipate how one might change the behavior of a commission plan.

The other way to make change less painful is to create data models and test commission plans as they are designed, and *before* they are put into production. Often, one of the most important steps in designing a commission plan is testing the plan. It's also one of the most overlooked steps because of the difficulty testing a plan properly.

Why is it important to test commission plans? Over the last twenty years as plans have become more innovative, they have also become much more complex. Variations, such as fast start and infinity commissions, have appeared, and new types of commission qualifications have been added.

The goal of any commission plan is to ensure that as a distributor's downline sales volume increases, his commissions also increase. But in some commission plans, as a distributor's downline grows and he begins to move between these commission types, a commission plan hits flat spots,—places where downline volume is growing but commissions are declining. A company needs to know this is going to happen before it opens for business so management can deal with it.

Many people wonder how you can test a commission plan. It isn't easy, because the only way to test a commission plan is with an actual distributor downline database. And even more importantly, that distributor downline must be built around the qualifications of the commission plan it's designed to test. Many companies try to test commissions using the same downline for every commission plan, but that simply can't work. If a commission plan rewards building wide, then you must have a downline database that is built wide; if a commission plan rewards building deep, then the database needs to be built differently. In addition, the orders in the database must be of the right size for the qualifications of the commission plan.

Enough distributors and orders must be created to test each commission type from simple retail commissions to overlapping infinity commissions reserved for the very top dream-builders. As a result of all of this, a company typically needs several thousand distributors with accompanying orders in a test downline, and run commissions for several months.

There are several benefits to testing a commission plan. The most important benefit is to find any flat spots, or other unexpected behaviors so a company can decide how it should fix them. The second advantage is that there is simply nothing like knowing that a commission plan does what you expect it to. It's amazing to realize how many network marketing companies have created great momentum and lost it never to get it back because their commission plan did not do what they expected it to do.

Two other benefits are the ability to fine-tune the plan and the ability to train corporate staff on how to explain and support the plan before the company opens for business.

Conclusion

I love network marketing because there is nothing like working side by side with people who are building a dream. But sometimes, we tend to overlook the strengths and weaknesses of a commission plan when moving toward our dream. Swept away by all the excitement, we don't step back and evaluate why some plans work and others don't.

The dream of network marketing is the dream of freedom, prosperity, autonomy, and flexibility. For this reason, it's time for those of us who have spent decades in the industry to step back and better understand what works and why, because without a commission plan that satisfies the needs of the distributors involved, the dream we all hope for is unachievable. And after all my years on the inside of the industry, every now and then I see the magic of the right commission plan matched with the right product and the right company at the right time. And that is a great thing to be a part of!

Section Three: Putting Everything Together

At one point in my life, I thought I would write a book on commission plan design. But then I realized that would be a little like writing a book on do-it-yourself brain surgery. So I settled on a more reasonable goal: trying to explain the basics of commission plans. I originally thought it would take maybe six weeks; two years later I am finally finished, and I didn't even touch on the important issue of creating a commission plan that's integrated with a company's marketing strategy, and creating a marketing strategy that interfaces with an integrated product line. If you're starting a company and you're new to running a network marketing company, you should invest some money with one of the industry consultants that can help you create an integrated *product-marketing-commission-sales* strategy. If you don't know one, we can recommend a couple of good consultants we've worked with in the past. Give us a call at InfoTrax (801-802-8729), or go to our web site (www.infotraxsys.com).

Also, InfoTrax sponsors an industry website MLM.com which contains lots of good information about starting and growing a network marketing company. Every week, MLM.com chooses a topic of interest to the industry and publishes a daily article from industry leaders on that topic. If you register on the site, you will receive an email summary of each day's article. Because we hate spam, we will never sell or give out your email address to anyone. We only use it to send you this daily article summary.

Now let's talk about what I hope you have gained from reading this book. If you are a distributor, obviously, you should now understand the basics of what goes into the design and implementation of commission plans for the network marketing industry. I hope that you feel informed enough to make intelligent choices about the commission plan you want for the company you want to join.

If you are a company owner or are thinking about starting a company, I've tried to give you an overview of commission plan design. I've explained the building blocks, I've pointed out the advantages and disadvantages of a variety of approaches to the process, and I've tried to warn you against the mistakes I've seen other network marketing companies make.

Does that mean that it should now be easy for you to say, "This is the best commission plan for my company"? No, of course not. But I hope this book gives you the information you need to keep you from accidentally creating and implementing a plan that may prove disastrous.

I wish you all the best in growing your company or your downline, recruiting the best distributors available, and helping them to build successful businesses. Network marketing offers a wonderful opportunity for personal and financial growth for its participants. It this book helps you maximize that opportunity as smoothly and effectively as possible, I'll feel like I accomplished what I set out to do.

Glossary of Terms

Key Topics

Binary 215
Breakage 215
Breakaway 215
Business center 215
CV 215
Coding commission 215
Commissions 215
Commission blocking 215
Commission plan 216
Compression 216
Consumers 216
Critical mass 216
Crossing the desert 216
Differential commission 216
Direct sales 217
Distributor 217
Downline 217
Dream-builders 217
DSA 217
Earnings emphasis 217
Enroller 217
First level 217
Forced structure 218
Front-end loading 218
Garage qualifying 218
Genealogy 218
GV 218
Infinity commission 218
Leg 219

Matrix 219
MLM 219
Network marketing 219
QP 219
Qualified 219
Paid rank 220
Pin rank. 220
Product evangelists 220
Rank 220
Remote sponsoring. 220
Reversion 220
Rules 220
Sales leaders 221
Sponsor. 221
Sponsoring regulation. 221
Stacking 221
Structure. 221
Tree 221
Unilevel. 221
Upline 221

Glossary of Terms

Binary

A type of commission plan that requires a distributor to have two organizations with approximately equal sales volume.

Breakage

Money that doesn't get paid out in the commission plan because of unqualified distributors, too few levels, or some other reason. This money usually reverts to the company as profit.

Breakaway

A plan that allows an organization that reaches a certain level to break away from under its sponsor and move up in the tree.

Business center

Some commission plans allow multiple occurrences of a distributor in a tree. Each of these occurrences is known as a business center.

CV

Commission volume.

Coding commission

A commission plan that locks people into being paid commissions on the level at which a recruit first generated sales volume, regardless of the rise in rank of that recruit. The recruiter continues to be paid at that same level, regardless of the rank either may attain.

Commissions

A method by which earnings are distributed between the distributor and his or her upline: one component of a commission plan. Most companies have several types of commissions: for example, unilevel and infinity.

Commission blocking

A type of commission whereby a distributor can have his commission blocked by a qualified distributor in his downline. A differential commission can be a blocked commission; a level commission is not. Earnings can go to

Appendix: A   215 zero overnight if a distributor's entire check is based on a commission that can be blocked.

Commission plan

The combination of rules, commission types, and structure that defines how distributor compensation is calculated and paid.

Compression

A mechanism for bypassing unqualified or inactive distributors when determining payout so that the upline is paid on the number of active levels. Only active distributors count as levels in the commission plan.

Consumers

Those people who wish to purchase your products, but don't feel comfortable being product evangelists.

Critical mass

The point at which distributors begin making enough money to change their lifestyles, thereby providing a compelling reason to continue building the business.

Crossing the desert

The period of time during which distributors have not achieved critical mass; that is, the compensation they receive for the hours they spend is not letting them make more money than they could in other endeavors. All that keeps them going is the dream of reaching critical mass. Your commission plan needs to bring them to their desired income level before they become discouraged and quit.

Differential commission

A type of commission whereby a distributor receives the difference between the amount for which he qualifies and the amount for which his first level distributor qualifies. For example, if Distributor A qualifies for ten percent and his first level Distributor B qualifies for five percent, then Distributor A receives five percent.

Glossary of Terms

Direct sales

A method of distributing product that employs independent contractors who earn their commissions only on their own sales and not on the people they recruit into the business.

Distributor

A person or entity that has submitted a complete application and agreement, which your company has accepted.

Downline

The organizational descendants of a distributor on down to the bottom of the tree.

Dream-builders

Those distributors who have the drive and ambition to take them to the top of a network marketing organization. Your company needs such people in order to succeed, because they motivate their downlines and push up revenues.

DSA

Direct Selling Association. An organization that helps the non-traditional sales environment function in effective and ethical ways. For more information, check their web site at www.dsa.org.

Earnings emphasis

Occurs when a commission plan emphasizes a specific range of commission check sizes in conjunction with the company's overall marketing strategy.

Enroller

A "second sponsor" to whom part of the commission can be paid. This allows a distributor to place someone in her downline and still remain as that person's enroller, or second sponsor, and receive part of the commissions on that person.

First level

Those people directly under a distributor in the tree, or those whom he or she has personally recruited.

Appendix: A 217

Forced structure

A structure that distributors must adhere to in order to receive commissions or advance in rank: for example, they must have an organization that is three distributors wide and three deep. A limited width structure allows for an organization only a certain number wide on the first level; a required width structure, open the other hand, makes the distributor responsible for having at least a certain number of distributors on the first level.

Front-end loading

Also known as garage qualifying. This is an unethical practice in which distributors and companies sell excess inventory to their downlines to receive more commission. Hence, the distributors fill up their garages with products that they can never use or sell. Many companies have been destroyed by front-end loading practices. In an effort to curb this practice, the DSA created a standard policy of allowing the distributors to return any resalable product to the company within one year of purchase.

Garage qualifying

See "front-end loading."

Genealogy

A distributor's downline is sometimes referred to as his or her genealogy.

GV

Group Volume. Companies that use group volume as a qualification have a rank in their commission plan that is defined as a group or leader rank. It's also often called a "breakaway" rank because it's earned when the distributor breaks away from his sponsor's group. In most companies, a distributor's group volume includes anyone for whom he is the first upline distributor who has not achieved this group rank.

Infinity commission

A type of commission in which a distributor is paid on all volume in his organization down to the next person with the same rank.

Glossary of Terms

Leg

A portion of a distributor's organization starting at one of his first level distributors and encompassing their entire organization. If a distributor has ten first level distributors, he has ten legs.

Matrix

A type of plan characterized by a limited width structure and normally paid in a unilevel-type payout.

MLM

Multilevel marketing. "MLM" actually refers to a compensation type within the network marketing industry. An MLM company uses a method of distributing product that allows its distributors not only to sell product, but also to recruit other distributors and then receive commissions on at least two levels of their downline activities. See "network marketing."

Network marketing

Another term for MLM, often preferred because it doesn't carry the negative connotations that the term "MLM" picked up because of the unsavory practices of a few participants. However, I believe MLM is actually a compensation type within the network marketing industry. See "MLM."

QP

Qualifying Points, one of the four standard prices on a product price list. Each company has its own name for QP; BV – business value, PV- Point value are two of the common variations. QP is used to calculate the qualifications for a commission plan. For example, when a commission plan has a qualification of 100 personal sales volume, it is 100 QPs. The primary reason companies use QP is that it allows for international commission plans and commission plan flexibility.

Qualified

A distributor who has met all the requirements necessary to be paid a commission.

Paid rank

The rank at which the distributor is qualified to be paid for the current month

Pin rank

The distributor's current rank, which may be higher than their paid rank

Pool commission A commission plan designed to reward leaders. A certain percentage of sales—for example, one percent—is set aside in a pool; this money is distributed to all who achieve a certain goal set by the company.

Product evangelists

Consumers of your product who are enthusiastic about your product and who bring you new consumers and new distributors, but who prefer to let the salespeople do the selling and signing up.

Rank

The title a distributor has earned in the organization by the sale of products or the building of an organization. Typically, a higher rank entitles a distributor to higher percentages.

Remote sponsoring

Sponsoring a distributor over a long distance, rather than person to person. All sponsoring and supporting activities are conducted via mail or electronically.

Reversion

When a distributor fails to qualify for certain rewards for a selected period of time, the distributor may lose his rank or part of his organization. That demotion is called "reversion" because the distributor reverts to a lower level.

Rules

The qualifications for the activities of selling and recruiting that a distributor must abide by in order to achieve ranks or receive commissions: one component of a commission plan.

Glossary of Terms

Sales leaders

The people who handle all the administrative aspects of recruiting and downline training and management, taking over these aspects from the product evangelists. Sales leaders deal with the people brought by the product evangelists.

Sponsor

A distributor's immediate upline.

Sponsoring regulation

A rule that defines who a distributor can recruit and under what conditions. For example, a company may have a regulation that forbids recruiting anyone under 18.

Stacking

A method by which some distributors attempt to beat the system by recruiting everyone whose name they can enter, planning to be paid a higher percentage because of the high number of recruits. This practice usually backfires, because the distributor must then generate sales to back up all these names.

Structure

The specific set of rules in commission plans that determine where people are placed in the organization: one component of a commission plan.

Tree

The hierarchy of sponsors and their downlines that comprises the organization.

Unilevel

A type of commission plan that pays percentages on personal or group volume, going so many levels deep in the organization.

Upline

A distributor's sponsor and then that person's sponsor and so on, all the way up to the top of the tree.

Understanding Multi-Level Commissions

Mark Rawlins Bio

Mark Rawlins is an innovator, an entrepreneur, and a technical leader for computer systems in the network marketing industry. His knowledgeable counsel has helped several network marketing companies to success, including Nikken Incorporated, Quorum, and Enrich. His influence has benefited not only individual companies, but also the industry as a whole.

Rawlins' knowledge of commission plans comes from the inside. "I've worked in the middle of the fastest-growing—and fastest-dying—companies in the business," he says. "I've seen all kinds of growth patterns. As a consultant, I've even been given beds at client companies while we worked through some of the problems that come with exponential growth."

Rawlins has a unique perspective on the network marketing industry in general and on commission plans in particular. "I like to listen to what the distributors say about their experiences," he says. "I like the fun and the excitement of a network marketing company. I enjoy watching the operations, even the details, like seeing the checks being printed. I like writing software that solves the problems I see cropping up. I've seen the crushing blows that can strike a company that was not prepared for rapid growth, and I enjoy having a hand in finding and conquering all kinds of mistakes in setting up commission plans. After all, an intelligent plan for distributor payout is at the heart of network marketing success." Rawlins says he finds the industry "maddening, exhausting, and fascinating."

You can find Mark Rawlins' company, InfoTrax, on the web at www.infotraxsys.com.

A Unique Perspective—Mark's Own

You may wonder who I am, and how I've come to understand these issues. I've worked in network marketing since 1981, and I've seen the rise and fall of many companies. I have more than twenty years of experience under my belt in helping people start and manage network marketing companies. My team and I have created software that has been used by more than 200 such companies. In 1988, we created the first voicemail and telephone touchtone order entry designed for this industry. At the beginning of the Internet revolution in 1995, we created a complete integrated suite of tools to help distributors order product, sign up other distributors, check worldwide volume, and generally manage their business on the Internet. We didn't simply create packaged software; rather, we created software solutions that addressed the real needs of operating network marketing companies. I've spent years working inside many network marketing companies, designing software systems to meet their specific needs. I've lived through their hyper-growth. My team and I have worked round the clock for weeks on end to make certain our client companies can pay their distributors in a timely and reliable manner. I've worked with many of the successful startup network marketing companies to appear during the last twenty years.

I've been fascinated by watching companies try to solve their problems by changing their commission plans. Sometimes the changes work and send the company to new heights. At other times, the unintended and unanticipated consequences can be massive, changing fairly minor problems into full-blown disasters.

Great field leaders must believe in the plan. If they don't believe in it, they can't sell it. If they can't sell it, the company is out of business. I can't emphasize too strongly how important it is for a company to build a plan that's enthusiastically supported by its field leadership.

I look at network marketing not from the sales aspect, but from the operational aspect. I've observed the operations of many companies, and I've done a great deal of analysis on why things work the way they do. I've thought a great deal about why some of the companies I worked with went on to become highly successful, while others seemed to simply dry up and blow away. In the process of all this work, study, and analysis, I've come to some pretty interesting conclusions—conclusions that I believe can help you steer through the rough shoals of commission plan design, and I've tried to include them in this book.

Understanding Multi-Level Commissions

InfoTrax and Distributor Confidence

Key Topics

InfoTrax Systems.. 229
  DataTrax BackOffice....................................... 230
  NetTrax VirtualOffice...................................... 230
  Integrated Communication Tools 231
  WebMeeting Module 231
  Voice Messaging Module................................... 231
Conclusion 232

Understanding Multi-Level Commissions

InfoTrax and Distributor Confidence

> From athletics to business, it's amazing how confidence determines success or failure. Consider the Michael Jordan era with the Chicago Bulls or the emergence of HP from the garage under the leadership of Hewlett and Packard. Each built confidence within the organization through the flawless execution of process and the tireless pursuit of their vision. Individual confidence is the cornerstone of championship teams and enduring corporations.

At InfoTrax Systems, every system we deploy is measured by its ability to ensure distributor confidence and create operational efficiencies within your direct sales business. We enable our clients to build and support the relationship between the corporate office and distributors in the field.

At each new stage of your business, our integrated account management teams will provide personalized service and dedicated multi-tier support, to ensure confidence in your business processes and systems for even your newest distributor. This approach, combined with our experience and technology, enable you to make autonomous business decisions specific to your objectives and implement proven technology solutions.

InfoTrax Systems

InfoTrax focuses on the direct sales industry and through our employees provide the know-how and industry experience to ensure your company's success. Our staff has over 200 years of combined experience in the direct sales industry. By creating accurate and efficient business operations through the design and automation of our clients' business processes, our clients experience proven results in:

1. Distributor growth and retention
2. Increased revenue per employee ratios
3. Measurable returns on technology investment

Managing the growth of your company is critical to your long-term success. Last year, InfoTrax clients received and processed more than one million orders over the Internet. Presently, our largest client conducts eighty percent of its business transactions (orders, support, customer service, and so on) using automated processes.

DataTrax BackOffice

The heart of InfoTrax's product offering is DataTrax. With more than 450 built-in routines and programs, DataTrax provides integrated systems for distributor tracking and maintenance, order processing, inventory management, order fulfillment, warehouse automation, commission processing, and distributor management systems. DataTrax is easy to use, yet scalable to manage rapidly growing businesses. And with DataTrax's personalization layer, you can easily customize the software without locking into a specific version (Rev Lock). DataTrax is also available in a hosted model, eliminating the need for upfront hardware and software investment.

NetTrax VirtualOffice

An online environment for real-time distributor information and e-commerce is critical to your distributors. And that is exactly what NetTrax VirtualOffice gives your distributor base: powerful, online business management tools, real-time access to down-line genealogy and reporting, new distributor sponsoring (personal web pages), product ordering (shopping cart), package tracking, online applications, down-line activity alerts, and more. All transactions seamlessly integrate with your DataTrax back office system for instant business-building information. The result is increased distributor confidence through real-time information and control, and applications designed specifically for your business that generates higher revenues and productivity.

The online environment created through NetTrax allows distributors to manage their business 24/7. Anywhere at anytime, the distributor can enroll new distributors, take product orders, edit personal information, access personal and group volume information, view genealogy, track packages, access their communications, and manage their business.

Integrated Communication Tools

Using the InfoTrax Systems communication tools enables you to communicate accurately and efficiently with every distributor in the field, from the corporate or distributor level. From prospecting to internal communications with your organization, the real key is that cost is dramatically reduced in comparison to traditional conference calling or on site meetings. Our goal is to eliminate time and distance limitations for training and recruiting, while providing personal interaction for the participants.

WebMeeting Module

The cornerstone is WebMeeting, our multi-media web-casting module. WebMeeting combines voice, live interaction, and multimedia presentations to provide interactive, two-way communications, optimized for the home dial-up/modem market. WebMeeting enables your business leaders and builders to train your new distributors and provide live conferencing with multi-media options, and then archive those conferences for the future. With WebMeeting, distributors can effectively recruit and prospect anywhere in the world with live multi-media presentations. Upline leaders will have the ability to empower new distributors immediately with ready-made presentations.

Voice Messaging Module

Nothing is more important to business building than communication within the organization. That's why InfoTrax designed our integrated voice response system exclusively for the direct sales industry. Your distributors will appreciate personal communications and a powerful recruiting tool. The system includes personal toll or toll free numbers, voice messaging, fax on demand, IVR order entry and sponsoring and free online messaging. When integrated with DataTrax, the IVR tool also empowers users with on-the-phone transactions and account information.

These tools, specifically built for your distributors and their business, will automate your distributor communications, while providing distributors with powerful multimedia presentation and recruiting tools.

Conclusion

At each stage of your business, you will break new ground in distributor growth and total orders processed while setting new records for sales and revenues. We've been there before, and we look forward to being there with you and ensuring your success. Confidence is fragile; handle with care!

For more information on any InfoTrax solution, visit our web site at www.infotraxsystems.com, e-mail us at sales@infotraxsystems.com, or call us at (801) 802-8729.

Commission Plan Payout: Exercises

Key Topics

Paying Commissions with a Unilevel Commission plan 236
Unilevel with No Compression............................... 238
   Example 1 238
   Example 2 240
Unilevel with Standard Compression, Examples 3 and 4 242
   Example 3 242
   Example 4 244
Unilevel Standard Compression, Examples 5 and 6 245
   Example 5 246
   Example 6 248
Unilevel with Dynamic Compression, Examples 7 and 8 249
   Example 7 250
   Example 8 252
Stairstep Differential 254
   Example 1 255
   Example 2 257
   Example 3 258
   Example 4 259

Understanding Multi-Level Commissions

Commission plan Payout: Exercises

In this section, we will go over a lot of exercises relating the payout of different commission plans and scenarios. Each exercise has a graphic associated with it that shows a single downline. These distributors are all part of the larger tree structure of the company. This example of the "tree" shows this concept. These distributors are not working in a vacuum; they're part of a larger picture. We have taken only one distributor with a purchase and worked up the tree to illustrate commission payout.

Figure a

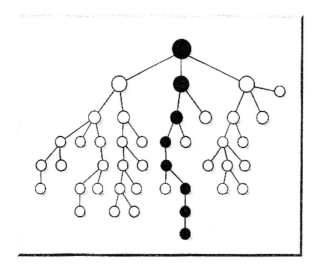

Understanding Multi-Level Commissions

Paying Commissions with a Unilevel Commission plan

Figure b

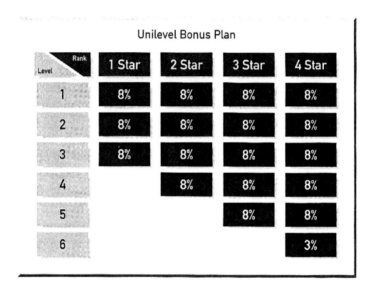

This chart shows you how distributors in a unilevel plan might be paid according to rank and level.

One reason companies have problems with their commission plans is that they tend to figure compensation from the *top down*. That's what they do when they draw their circles, and that's why they produce a skewed version of the results!

To avoid problems, you need to figure compensation from the *bottom up*. In this section, we'll walk you through enough payout processes that you'll have this concept well in mind by the time we finish.

We're going to assume a hypothetical network marketing company: Acme Widgets. We'll look at how its commission plan might work, using several different methods of calculating distributor commissions.

First, let's look at a unilevel commission plan that pays out according to the chart in Figure b. Note that distributors may be paid different percentages on different levels, or they may receive more if they've earned higher ranks.

In this example, we'll move step by step through the payout on two different distributors, each placing a $100 order. Note that we'll be moving *up the tree*, starting with the distributor who placed the order under discussion. We'll examine the payout results when we use *no compression*, when we apply *standard compression*, and when we apply *dynamic compression*.

The chart tracks payout for each distributor by name. You can see exactly how commissions on each distributor's sales volume are calculated and disseminated. The distributor's rank is next to his or her name. This rank may affect the percentage the distributor receives for sales in his or her downline. An "X" in the circle indicates that the distributor is not qualified to receive a commission.

By the name of each of the five distributors who places an order is the notation "PV 100" to indicate a personal volume of $100.

Understanding Multi-Level Commissions

Unilevel with No Compression

Let's step through the payout process on several distributors, starting with Marcus.

Example 1

Figure c

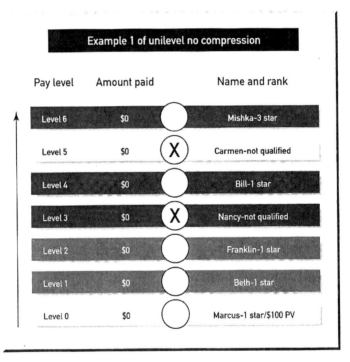

1. Marcus, whose rank is 1-Star, places an order for $100. (Start at the bottom of the chart with the circle for Marcus. We'll be moving *up* the tree for each transaction. The rank of 1-Star is the lowest rank.) Distributors are not paid on their own volume, so this transaction counts as level 0.

2. We then go up the tree to Marcus's sponsor, Beth. (Note by the number in the circle that Beth holds the rank of 1-Star.) Beth is qualified to receive commissions. (She probably

Commission Plan Payout: Exerceses

generated enough sales herself in order to qualify, or she may have recruited a certain number of distributors in order to qualify.) Since Beth is one level up from the person who made the sale, also known as the *pay matrix*, she earns eight percent—in this case, $8.

3. Next we go up the tree to Beth's sponsor, Franklin, who is ranked 1-Star and qualified to receive commissions. Franklin is two levels up from Marcus and is therefore entitled to eight percent, or $8 again in this case, because a qualified 1-Star is paid on three levels. (See Figure b.)

4. Going up to level 3, we come to Cecily, who is not qualified to receive commissions this month. Cecily, then, receives $0.

5. Next up the tree is Bill, who is a qualified 1-Star and is four levels up from Marcus. When we look at the chart in Figure b, we see that 1-Stars are paid only on three levels. Therefore, poor Bill makes zero percent on Marcus's sales volume.

6. Now we move up the tree to Carmen. Even if she has a high enough rank to be paid five levels deep, she isn't qualified to receive commissions, and therefore is paid $0. Carmen may not have felt like selling widgets this month.

7. The next distributor up the tree is Mishka, who is a qualified 3-Star. 3-Stars are paid down only five levels. Because we're at level 6, she receives $0.

Now let's trace the payout on another distributor's personal sales volume.

Appendix: D

Example 2

Figure d

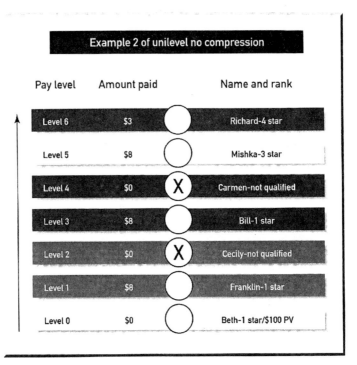

1. Beth places an order for $100. (You can find this distributor's circle just above that for Marcus in the tree.) Since distributors are not paid on their own volume, it counts as level 0.

2. Beth's sponsor, next up the tree, is Franklin, who is a qualified 1-Star and is therefore, as you see in Figure b, paid $8 at level 1.

3. Next up the tree is Cecily, who is not qualified to receive commissions and therefore is paid $0 at level 2 (meaning the second level up from the distributor who made the sale).

4. Now move on up the tree to Bill, who is a qualified 1-Star. This distributor is therefore paid $8 at level 3. (Figure b tells you that 1-Stars are paid on three levels.)

5. Next we come to Carmen, who is, alas, unqualified and so receives $0.

6. Then we move up the tree to Mishka, a qualified 3-Star. 3-Stars are paid on five levels, so Mishka is paid $8 at level 5.

7. Finally, we reach Richard who, as a qualified 4-Star, is paid $3 at level 6. (See the chart in Figure b to see that the payout for level 6 drops from eight percent to three percent.)

If all possible commission payments with this unilevel plan were paid, the plan would pay $43 on each of the $100 orders we traced, for a total of $86. The total paid in this example, however, is only $43, because in each case some distributors were not qualified to receive their commissions. The remainder, $43, is retained by the company as profit.

Understanding Multi-Level Commissions

Unilevel with Standard Compression, Examples 3 and 4

Now let's look at the effect that standard compression has on payout. With standard compression, an unqualified distributor does not count as a level. Because unqualified levels are skipped over, commissions can be paid to distributors at additional levels up the tree.

This example we're going to step through involves the same tree, ranks, qualifications, and orders that we used in the previous example. The only difference is that we apply standard compression to the payout process.

Example 3

Figure e

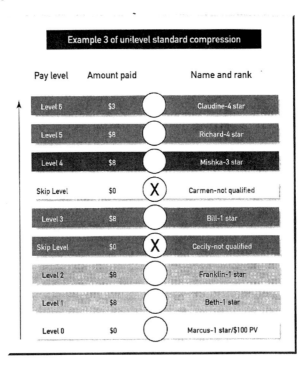

1. Marcus places an order for $100. (Start at the bottom of the chart with the circle for Marcus. We'll be moving up the tree

Commission Plan Payout: Exerceses

for each transaction.) Distributors are not paid on their own volume, so it counts as level 0.

2. We then go up the tree to Marcus's sponsor, Beth. (Note by the number in the circle that Beth holds the rank of 1-Star.) Beth is qualified to receive commissions. Since Beth is one level up from the pay matrix, she earns eight percent—in this case, $8.

3. Next we go up the tree to Beth's sponsor, Franklin, who is ranked 1-Star and qualified to receive commissions. Franklin is two levels up from the pay matrix and is therefore entitled to eight percent, or $8 again.

4. Next up the tree is Cecily, who is not qualified to receive commissions this month and is therefore paid $0. The level is now level 3, but because she is unqualified, the level does not change to the next upline.

5. Next up the tree is Bill, a qualified 1-Star. Because Cecily is not qualified, that level was skipped, leaving Bill only three levels up from Marcus. When we look at the chart in Figure b, we see that 1-Stars are paid eight percent on three levels. That means that Bill makes $8 on Marcus's $100 sales volume.

6. Now we come to Carmen. We're now at level 4. Carmen, who is not qualified, is paid $0 and the level does not change.

7. The next upline is Mishka, who is a qualified 3-Star, paid down five levels. Because of compression, we're still at level 4. Mishka receives $8.

8. Next up the tree is Richard, who is a qualified 4-Star and is paid $8 at level 5.

9. Then we move up to level 6 for Claudine, who is also a qualified 4-Star. She is paid $3 because a qualified 4-Star receives three percent on sales volume generated six levels down.

Appendix: D

Understanding Multi-Level Commissions

Note that now all of the $43 commission was paid, whereas without compression only $16 was paid.

Now let's trace the payout on Beth's sales volume of $100.

Example 4

Figure f

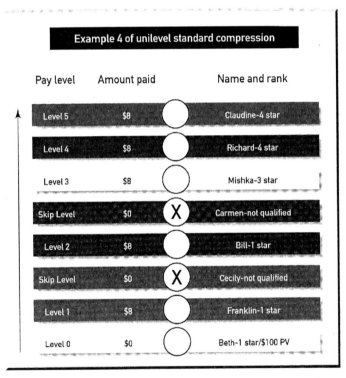

1. Beth places an order for $100. Distributors are not paid on their own volume, so it counts as level 0.

2. Beth's sponsor is Franklin, who as a qualified 1-Star is paid $8 at level 1.

3. Now we move up the tree to Cecily, who is unqualified to receive commissions and is paid $0 at level 2. The level does not change.

4. Next up the tree is Bill, who is a qualified 2-Star and is therefore paid $8 at level 2.

5. Now we come to Carmen, who is unqualified and is therefore paid $0.

6. Then we go up the tree to Mishka, who is a qualified 3-Star and is paid $8 at level 3.

7. Now we move up the tree to Richard, who as a qualified 4-Star, is paid $8 at level 4.

8. At last we reach Claudine, a qualified 4-Star, who receives $8 on level 5.

Note that $40 was paid this time, whereas $27 was paid without compression. Because unqualified distributors don't count as levels, commissions can be paid to distributors at additional levels up the tree. However, if the payout level reaches the top of the tree, any commission that remains is profit to the company.

If all commissions from this unilevel plan were paid, the plan would pay $43 on each of the above orders for a total of $86. The total paid in this example is $83. The remainder of $3 is retained by the company. Note that applying compression to the payout process gives more to the distributors at the top of the tree because unqualified distributors drop out of the tree for commission purposes.

Unilevel Standard Compression, Examples 5 and 6

This example uses the same tree and the same orders that the previous example used. However, we've changed the ranks and qualifications. We've made these changes so we can show you standard compression with this tree. Then, when you examine the examples that use dynamic compression, you'll be able to see the difference.

Understanding Multi-Level Commissions

Let's begin by tracing payout for good old Marcus.

Example 5

Figure g

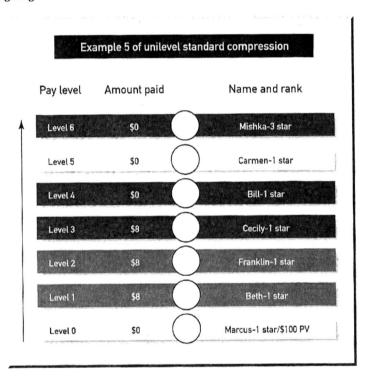

1. Marcus places an order for $100. (Start at the bottom of the chart with the circle for Marcus. We'll be moving up the tree for each transaction.) Distributors are not paid on their own volume, so it counts as level 0.

2. We then go up the tree to Marcus's sponsor, Beth. (Note by the number in the circle that Beth's rank is 1-Star.) Beth is qualified to receive commissions. Since Beth is one level up from the pay matrix, she earns eight percent—in this case, $8.

3. Next we go up the tree to Beth's sponsor, Franklin, who is a 1-Star and qualified to receive commissions. Franklin is two levels up from the pay matrix and is therefore entitled to eight percent, or $8 again in this case.

4. Next up the tree is Cecily, who is a qualified 1-Star and so is paid $8. The level is now 3.

5. Next up the tree is Bill, who is a qualified 1-Star and is four levels up from Marcus. When we look at the chart, we see that 1-Stars are paid on only three levels. Therefore, Bill makes $0 on Marcus.

6. Now we move up to up to Carmen, who is a 1-Star and qualified. We're now at level 5. Carmen is paid $0, because 1-Stars are only paid through three levels.

7. Next up the tree is Mishka, who is a qualified 3-Star. 3-Stars are paid on only five levels. Because we're at level 6, this distributor receives $0.

8. At level 6, the payout stops.

Now let's track Beth, who is a level up from Marcus.

Understanding Multi-Level Commissions

Example 6

Figure h

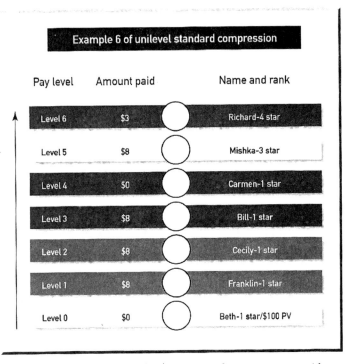

1. Beth places an order for $100. Distributors are not paid on their own volume, so it counts as level 0.

2. Beth's sponsor is Franklin, who, as a qualified 1-Star, is paid $8 at level 1.

3. Now we move up the tree to Cecily, who is qualified and a rank 1-Star. She is paid $8 at level 2.

4. Moving up the tree, we come to Bill, a qualified 1-Star, who is paid $8 at level 3.

5. Next, we come to Carmen, who is a qualified 1-Star. This rank entitles a distributor to receive commissions on three levels only, so, at level 4, Carmen is paid $0.

6. Then we move up the tree to Mishka, who is a qualified 3-Star and is therefore paid $8 at level 5.

7. Finally, we come to Richard, who, as a qualified 4-Star, is paid $3 at level 6.

By this time you should be clear on how a unilevel commission plan calculates commissions when applying standard compression.

If all of the commissions from the plan in these examples were paid, the plan would pay $43 on each of the above orders for a total of $86. The total paid in this example is $59 and the remainder of $27 is retained by the company.

Unilevel with Dynamic Compression, Examples 7 and 8

This example uses the same tree, ranks, qualifications, and orders that we used with the previous example. We're going to show the application of dynamic compression with this tree. With *dynamic compression*, you not only skip a level for each unqualified distributor, but you also skip a level for each distributor who wasn't paid. For example, a distributor may have been qualified for commissions that month, but didn't have the rank to enable him to be paid on his level.

Let's trace the same orders through the tree, but this time, notice what changes occur in the payout because of dynamic compression. Much of what occurs is the same as you've seen before, so watch carefully for the differences and their effects.

Example 7

Figure i

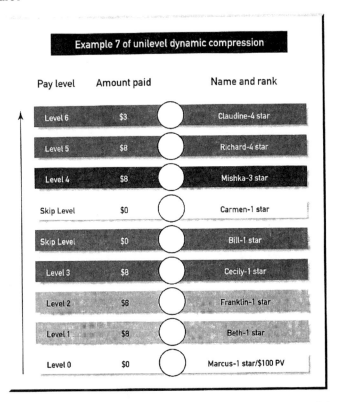

1. Marcus places an order for $100. (Start at the bottom of the chart with the circle for Marcus. We'll be moving up the tree for each transaction.) Distributors are not paid on their own volume, so it counts as level 0.

2. We then go up the tree to Marcus's sponsor, Beth, who is a rank 1-Star. Beth is qualified to receive commissions. Since Beth is one level up from the pay matrix, she earns eight percent—in this case, $8.

3. Next we go up the tree to Beth's sponsor, Franklin, who is a 1-Star and qualified to receive commissions. Franklin is two

levels up from the pay matrix and is therefore entitled to 8 percent, or again $8.

4. Next up the tree is Cecily, who is qualified and is therefore paid $8. The level is now 3, because there has been no reason so far to skip a level.

5. Next we come to Bill, who is a qualified 1-Star, four levels up from Marcus. When we look at the chart in Figure b, we see that 1-Stars are paid on three levels only. Therefore, Bill makes $0 on Marcus. Because the payout was 0, the level stays the same.

6. Now we move up the tree to Carmen, who is qualified. We're still at level 4; Carmen is paid $0 because 1-Stars are paid only on three levels. Therefore, the level stays the same for the next upline.

7. The next person up the tree is Mishka, who is a qualified 3-Star, and therefore paid down five levels. Because we're at level 4, Mishka receives $8 and the level increases to level 5.

8. Next up the tree is Richard, who is a qualified 4-Star and is paid $8 at level 5.

9. Then we move up to Claudine, who is a qualified 4-Star and is paid $3 at level 6.

10. We're now at level 6, so the payout stops.

Now let's move on to Beth.

Example 8

Figure j

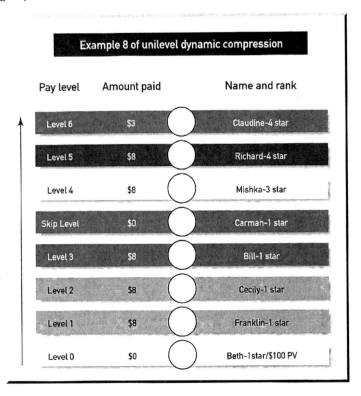

1. Beth places an order for $100. Distributors are not paid on their own volume, so it counts as level 0.

2. Beth's sponsor is Franklin, who, as a qualified 1-Star, is paid $8 at level 1.

3. Now we move up the tree to Cecily, who is qualified and is paid $8 at level 2.

4. Next we come to Bill, who is a qualified 1-Star and is therefore paid $8 at level 3.

5. Now we come to Carmen, who is a qualified 1-Star at level 4. Since 1-Stars are paid on only three levels, this distributor is paid $0, even though qualified to receive commissions. Because the payout is zero, the level does not change. This is the difference between standard and dynamic compression.

6. Then we move up to Mishka, who is a qualified 3-Star. She is paid $8 at level 4.

7. Now we come to Richard, who, as a qualified 4-Star, is paid $8 at level 5.

8. Finally, we move on to Claudine, who is a qualified 4-Star and is paid $3 at level 6. At level 6, the payout stops.

If all of the commissions from this unilevel plan were paid, the plan would pay $43 on each of the above orders for a total of $86. The total paid in this example is $86. Note that applying dynamic compression results in a payout of $27 more than applying standard compression in examples 5 and 6 yields.

Stairstep Differential

Figure k

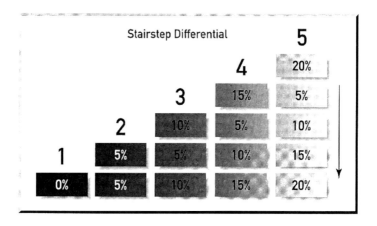

This chart shows the payout in terms of ranks for a stairstep differential commission plan.

With a differential commission, a certain percentage of profit is available for commission payments, and this amount must be distributed. As I pointed out in Chapter Four, most differential commission plans are stairsteps, in which distributor percentage increases with increasing levels of group volume (GV).

To read this chart, look at the percentage directly below your rank for the amount you will be paid on your own purchases. For example, a Rank 1 is paid zero percent on his own purchases, but a Rank 2 is paid five percent on his personal orders. To see what you'll be paid on the distributors in your downline, you can look below your rank to the rank of your downline distributor. For example, a Rank 3 is paid ten percent on his own purchases. Then, moving downward, we see that he receives five percent on any Rank 2s and ten percent on any Rank 1s. Look at a Rank 5. You can see that a Rank 5 distributor earns twenty percent on his own purchases, five percent on a Rank 4 distributor, ten percent on a Rank 3 distributor, fifteen percent on a Rank 2 distributor, and twenty percent on a Rank 1 distributor.

Commission Plan Payout: Exerceses

Now that you have the basics for reading the chart, let's look at some examples on how to calculate the payout for this type of commission.

In this example of the stairstep differential compensation calculation, I show payout on four distributors, each with a $100 order. As with the earlier example, the chart shows the name and rank of each distributor. An "X" in the circle indicates that that distributor is not qualified to receive a commission. Each of the distributors who places an order is given the label "PV 100."

So let's step through the payout for each distributor.

Example 1

Figure l

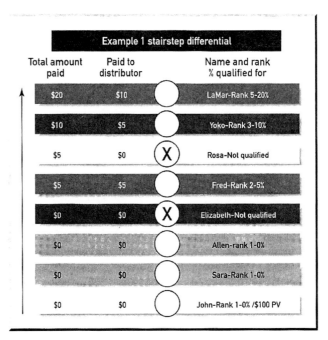

1. John places an order for $100. Because John is at Rank 1, he is paid zero percent, or $0, on his own order.

2. John's sponsor is Sara, who is also at Rank 1 and is paid $0.

3. Then we move up the tree to Alan, who is also Rank 1 and is therefore paid $0.

4. Next up the tree is Elizabeth, who is not qualified and so is paid $0.

5. Next we come to Fred, who is Rank 2 and paid $5.

6. Rosa comes next, but is not qualified and so is paid $0.

7. Then we reach Yoko, who is a qualified Rank 3. A Rank 3 distributor is paid ten percent. However, *because we've paid five percent already*, this distributor is paid the *difference*, which is $5.

8. Finally, LaMar is paid on this order as a qualified Rank 5. LaMar qualifies for twenty percent, but ten percent **has been paid already**, so we pay the *remaining* ten percent, or $10.

Now for Sara and the payout on her order.

Example 2

Figure m

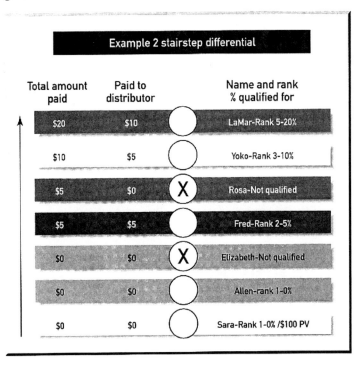

1. Sara places an order for $100. Because Sara is at Rank 1, she is paid zero percent, or $0, on her own order.

2. Then we move up the tree to Alan, who is also Rank 1 and thus paid $0.

3. Next up the tree is Elizabeth, who is not qualified and therefore receives nothing.

4. Next up the tree is Fred, who is Rank 2 and is therefore paid $5.

5. Rosa is next, but is not qualified and therefore receives nothing.

Understanding Multi-Level Commissions

6. Then we come to Yoko, who is a qualified 3-Star. Rank 3s are normally paid ten percent, but because we've paid five percent already, this distributor is paid the difference, which is $5.

7. Finally, LaMar is paid on this order as a qualified 5-Star. This rank normally qualifies for twenty percent, but we've already paid out ten percent, so we pay this distributor the remaining ten percent, or $10.

Example 3

Figure n

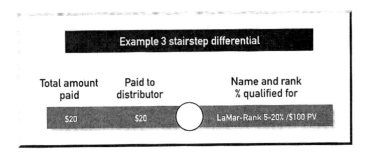

Here's a quick-and-simple example.

1. LaMar places an order for $100. Because LaMar is a 5-Star, this distributor is paid twenty percent, or $20, on his own order. Because all of the twenty percent has been paid, we stop paying.

This example about a different distributor's order shows the benefit of the stairstep plan to a distributor several steps from the actual order placement.

Commission Plan Payout: Exerceses

Example 4

Figure o

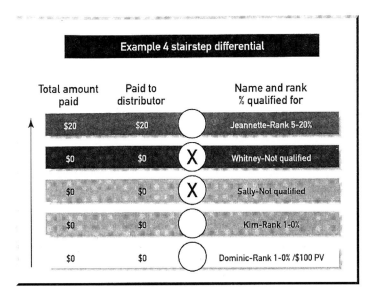

1. Dominic places an order for $100. Because Dominic is a Rank 1, he is paid zero percent, or $0, on his own order.

2. This distributor's sponsor is Kim, who is also a Rank 1 and therefore receives nothing.

3. The next two upline sponsors (Sally and Whitney) are not qualified. They therefore receive nothing.

4. Finally, we reach Jeannette, who is qualified for twenty percent. Since nothing has been paid so far, we pay the remaining $20, or all of the commission, to Jeannette.

Understanding Multi-Level Commissions

The Internet and Network Marketing

Understanding Multi-Level Commissions

The Internet and Network Marketing

Over the last few years we've seen the rise and retreat of the Internet. A couple of years ago, people said the Internet was going to change everything; now, it seems, people are saying that the Internet is not going to change anything, and all the dot-com companies are crashing. So what's the truth?

In my opinion, the truth is somewhere in the middle. For some industries, the Internet has drastically changed the process of their businesses. For companies that provide specific information to individuals, the Internet is extraordinarily important from both a cost and timeliness perspective to their business.

For our industry, I believe that the Internet will change network marketing more than all other communications services that have ever come along. The reason is that the Internet provides the mechanism for radically improving the communications between a company, the distributor, and the customer.

Our company invested in writing Internet software back in 1995, even before the law went into effect allowing the Web to be used for commercial ventures. At that time we wrote our first simple Internet product—one that allowed distributors to place orders, check volume, run genealogies, and perform a few other simple transactions. It's clear that the first obvious opportunities for the Internet, both then and now, were to allow the distributor to place orders twenty-four hours a day, to check on the status of those orders, and to receive sales reports.

Offering this ability gives a company two advantages. The first is that distributors are able to order at their own convenience and to get more information about the orders, making the process easier. The second advantage is a lower transaction cost to the company. If a customer checks on an order on the Internet, the company has just saved the cost of paying a customer service representative to take that call. In other words, this service allows the company to become more efficient and thereby lower its costs, which translates into the ability to spend more money on product development, lower prices, or raise commissions. Bottom line: it lowers the cost of operations.

Understanding Multi-Level Commissions

The next evolution of services starting to take hold in the Internet arena involves allowing customers to order directly, using retail shopping carts and other marketing services. Also included in this evolution are a number of communications and training services. One of the ongoing major challenges for network marketing companies is the need for effectively training and motivating the distributor. Companies can have conventions once a year, and perhaps hold regional conventions one other time each year. Unfortunately, this means that they really only have good contact with the distributors once or twice a year. **The Internet provides an opportunity for the company to be in contact with the distributor literally every day.**

In the summer of 2001, we launched a product called WebMeeting that allows a network marketing company to hold a virtual meeting every day. Top officials in the company can provide a voice broadcast, including multimedia slides that are available to the entire distributor force as often as they want! They can broadcast literally every day if they wish! WebMeeting is an easy-to-use, 24-hour business-building communicator that broadcasts a company's conference calls, training classes, success stories, and more over the Internet. In addition, it archives them online so customers, prospects, and downline members can listen to them...*anytime!* With this technique, a company can hold training classes every week. They don't have to fly people out. Companies spend millions of dollars each year on the travel expenses for training. Obviously, they can now substantially reduce these costs.

The third evolution of services for the Internet allows independent distributors to truly be **independent** distributors, able to access the kind of sales management reports that vice presidents of sales and sales managers have been getting for the last fifteen years from sophisticated computer systems. They also need to be truly able to manage their customers. They can provide for their customers a web page that not only enables product ordering, but also gives access to information that's important for each customer.

Now you say, "Are distributors going to want to do all this work?" The answer, of course, is "No." The distributors will be able to choose from profiles and templates, which the companies create and provide. Making these selections is similar to picking from the à la carte menu in a restaurant. A company doesn't need to provide a million different pages; rather, it supplies thirty different options from which distributors choose four or five. Although that's tens of thousands of different options, it's still easy to do.

This personalized page concept allows distributors to customize the information for their customers. This personalization strengthens the relationship between the distributor and the customer, at the same time allowing distributors to effectively support more customers.

A well-thought-out Internet strategy also strengthens the relationship between the company and the distributor. Services like WebMeeting facilitate that process. And as we evolve into a society in which more than fifty percent of Americans and over eighty-five percent of network marketers use the Internet on a regular basis, this type of customer service will be expected and demanded.

What about the other fifty percent? Traditional means will still be necessary in those cases, but for those on the Internet, quick and easy access to information and service can be a great business advantage. Although the fifty percent figure is the average for everyone in the U.S., over the last twelve to eighteen months, we've seen that many more than half of new distributors have Internet access. Network marketing companies have a very high adoption rate of technology-savvy distributors who use the Internet. This technology allows them to use the Internet like never before in conjunction with traditional methods like voice mail by allowing them to pick up their voice messages on the Internet. Now the Internet can become the backbone for unified voice mail along with other communications mechanisms. So the Internet becomes the hub for:

Administrative tools	Ordering, genealogy, customer service reports, package tracking
Communications tools	WebMeeting - training, motivational calls, prospecting calls
Customer retention	Facilitating the sales process – interest, information, order

So as we look at the Internet marketplace today, gone is the myth that a great domain name will produce millions. But in its place is the understanding and experience that the Internet is a powerful tool that will continue to create efficient operations and effective distribution of information.

Index

SYMBOLS

3x9 Structure 173
5x7 Structure 173

A

Administrative Tasks 20
Aloe Vera 14
Anti-oxidants 14
Anti-stacking 75, 106, 114
Attract Dream-builders 42
Australian 2-up 111, 112, 122
  Commission Types 122
  Gains Four Distributors 122
  Gives Up Two Distributors 122
  Sponsor 122
Authorized Distributors 145
Automobile 125
Automobile Shared Pool Commissions 126, 157
  Car Points 127
  Commission Qualifications 127
  Driving Billboards 126
  Group Volume 127
  Luxury Car 126
  Mary Kay's Pink Cadillac 126
  Pool Commissions 127
  Sales Leaders 126
  Sales Performance 126
  Sense of Commitment 126
Avon 154

B

Bait-and-switch 42
Balance 36
Balance of
  Sales Commissions 36
  Sales Management Commissions 36
Barriers-to-signup 27, 34, 49, 144
  Authorized Distributors 145
  Demonstration Kit 144
  Expensive Sales Kits 144
  Required Training 144
  Retail Markup 145
  Retail Sales Requirements 145
  Wholesale Price 145
Barriers-to-signup advantages of 145
Barriers-to-signup disadvantages of 146
Barriers-to-signup Strategy 135, 141, 147, 154
  Active Salespeople 141
  Commission Plan 145
  Committment 141
  Communications Strategy 145
  Direct Sales 145
  Dream-builders 145, 146
  Expensive Product Demonstration Kit 141
  High Monthly Personal Sales 141
  Marketing Strategy 145
  Party Plan Business 145
  Product Evangelists 146
  Required Ongoing Training 141
  Research Strategy 145
  Retail Commission 141
  Retail Consumers 141
  Retail Margin 145
  Sales Leaders 145, 146
  Salespeople 146
  Salesperson 145
  Salesperson - Hostess - Attendees 145

Big Dream 42
Binary 54, 112, 116, 117, 119, 154, 175, 215
Balanced Sales Volume 177
Commission Payout 177
Commissions Paid Weekly 175, 177
Commission Types 175
Dream-builders 178
Earnings 179
Enroller Tree 176
Internet 179
Limited Amount of Sales Volume 176
Limited Number of Levels 176
Low- to Mid-range Sales Management Commissions 175, 178
Market America 178
Maximum Payout 177
Mid- to High-end Sales Commissions 175, 178
Multi-center Downline Trees 175, 177
Payline 175
Placement 179
Pool Commissions 175
Product Evangelists 178
Sales Commissions 175
Sales Leaders 178
Sales Management Commissions 175
Salespeople 178
Sales Volume 175, 177
Sponsor 175
Strengths 178
Two First Levels 175
Two Legs 175, 177
Unlimited Amount of Sales Volume 176
Unlimited Number of Levels 176
Usana 178
Weaknesses 179
Welfare Mentality 179
Binary Hybrids 117
Blocking Commissions 63, 79, 81
Breakage 71, 72, 74, 215
Breakaway 85, 152, 153, 157, 215
Breakaway is Takeaway 159
Breakaway Rank 96
Build Deep 111
Build Wide 111
Business-building 16
  Consumer Relations 16
  Retail Consumer Programs 16
  Web-based Training 16
Business Center 119, 215
Business Models 154
  Party Plan Business 154
  Traditional Network Marketing Business 154
Business Value 219
BV. *See also* Business Value

C

Calculating Stairstep Differential Commissions 254
  Commission Payments 254
  Group Volume 254
Calculating Unilevel Commissions 237
  Unilevel with Dynamic Compression 249
  Unilevel with No Compression 238
  Unilevel with Standard Compression 242
Car Points 127
Cause 16
Changing People's Lives 16
Changing Sponsorship 106
  Downline Poaching 106

Index

Sponsor 106
Channels of Distribution 11
Coding Commission 111, 112, 121, 215
  Commission Plan Structure 121
  Differential Commissions 121
  Level Commissions 121
  Mistakes 121
  Permanent Code 121
  Personal Sales Volume 121
  Rank 121
  Rank Advancement 121
  Salesperson 121
  Sponsor 121
  Timing 121
  Top Rank 121
Commission Blocking 215
Commission Calculation 152
Commission Payout 50, 51, 62, 66, 72, 93, 151
  Mid-range Emphasis 200
Commission Percentages 49, 51, 62, 81
Commission Percentage Split 55
Commission Plan 3, 4, 7, 8, 22, 29, 30, 32, 33, 35, 36, 40, 42, 43, 47, 111, 180, 216
  Commission Types
    Binary 194
    Hybrid-unilevel Commission 194
    Stairstep 194
    Unigen 194
Commission Plan Design 49
Commission Plan Rules 39, 56, 93
  Be Consistent 94
  Be Fair 94
  Changing Sponsorship 106
  Changing the Rules 94
  Commission Payout 94
  Commission Percentages 94
  Commission Qualifications 94
  Commission Types 95
  Distributorship Terminations 106
  Ethical Behavior 93
  Ethical Problems 93
  Legal Problems 93
  Make Sense 94
  Monthly Qualification Rules 104
  Only One Distributor Per Household 106
  Product Buyback 106
  Qualification Rules 93
  Rank Advancement 93, 94
  The Carrot 93
  The Stick 93
Commission Plans purpose of 185
  Earnings Emphasis Commission Plan 185
  Sales Management Commissions 197
Commission Plan Structure 151
  Australian 2-up 111, 122
  Build Deep 111
  Build Wide 111
  Coding Commission 111, 112, 121
  Enroller Tree 112
  Limited Structure 111
  Limited-width Structure 112, 116
  Minimum Amount of Structure 112
  Minimum Number of Distributors 112
  Multi-center Downline Trees 111, 119
  Proper Downline Structure 112
  Qualified Distributors 112
  Qualified Sales Leaders 112
  Required Structure 111
  Required-width Structure 112, 114
  Sales Leaders 112
  Sales Volume 112

269

Sponsors and Enrollers 111
Structure Requirements types of 114
Commission Qualifications 34, 35, 56, 66, 209
Commissions 7, 19, 215
Commissions for Sales 193
　Barriers-to-signup 193
　Commission Types 193
　Retail Profit 193
　Sales Commission 193
　Targeted to Sales People 193
Commissions Paid Weekly 175
Commission Types 54, 56, 61, 62, 67, 77, 151, 155, 159, 172, 181, 209
　Binary Hybrids 117
Commission Value 136, 137
Communications 7, 16, 21, 30
Communication Strategy 4, 17, 18, 52
Community Events 37
Companies type of
　Barriers-to-signup 27, 49
　Direct Sales 5
　Direct Sales Company 4
　MLM 4
　Multi-level Marketing 4
　Network Marketing 5
　Open-enrollment 27, 49
　Party Plan Company 5
　Referral Marketing 167
　Sales-oriented 35
Company Mission 8, 16, 30, 39, 49, 206
Company Profitability 19
Compensation Calculation 236
　Bottom Up 236
　Top Down 236
Compensation Strategies 195
Competitive Advantage 207

Complexity of Commission Plan 118
Compression 66, 70, 96, 158, 216
　Breakage 71
　Commission Payout 70
　First-level Distributor 70
　Inactive Distributors 70, 71
　Level Commissions 70
　Non-qualified Distributors 70, 71
　Paid Rank 71
　Pin Rank 71
　Rank Advancement 71
　Rollup 74
　Terminate Distributor 71
Computers 20, 205
Computer Sales 15
Conference Calls 21, 199, 205
Consistency in Payout 34, 56, 58, 208
Consultants 4
Consumer Relations 16
Consumer Retention 29
Consumers 27, 28, 29, 31, 32, 33, 34, 37, 50, 52, 55, 56, 216
　Become Product Evangelists 194
　Buy One, Get One Free 194
　Differential Commissions 194
　Free Product for Referring 194
　Free Shipping 194
　Level Commissions 194
　One-time Referral Commission 194
　Open-enrollment 194
　Try New Products 194
　Two Commission Types 194
Consumer Service 142
Consumer Socio-economic Profile 9
Cost of Consumer Acquisition 9
Conventions 16, 37, 58
Cornerstones of Network Marketing Company
　Commissions 7
　Communications 7

Index

Product 7
Services 7
Corporate Philosophy 17
Critical Mass 216
Crossing the Desert 174, 216
Cruises 58
CV. *See also* Commission Value

D

Data Models 209
Day Job 40
Demographics 27
Demonstration Kit 144
Differential Commission 216
Differential Commissions 61, 75, 89, 157, 181
  Blocking Commissions 81
  Commission Payout 75
  Commission Percentages 77, 81
  Commission Types 77, 81
  Dream-builders 76
  Group Volume 76
  Overlapping Infinity 76
  Promotion Methods 81
  Break on the Fly 82
  Qualify/Effective Month 82
  Start Over 82
  Rank 77
  Rank Advancement 81
  Sales Leaders 76
  Sales Management Commissions 76
  Salesperson 76
  Sponsor 77
  Stacking 81
  Stairstep 76, 78
  Stepped Infinity 79
  Strong Points 80
  Target a Specific Activity 76

Target Earnings 75
Unilevel Commission 75
Weakness of 81
Differentiation 16
Direct Mailings 5
Direct Sales 3, 4, 5, 7, 10, 217, 229
Direct Selling Association 4, 5, 106
Discount Superstore 11, 206
Distributor 217
Distributor Behavior 35, 56
Distributor Loyalty 58
Distributors 4, 5, 8, 27
Distributorship Terminations 106
Distributor Wholesale Price 142
Double Breakaways 180
Downline 217
Downline Commissions 35
Downline Poaching 106
Downline Rank Achievements 96
Downline Sales 41
Downline Volume 209
Downloadable Documents 207
Dr. Arthur Laffer Economist 50
Dream-builders 19, 28, 30, 31, 32, 42, 56, 61, 66, 67, 105, 210, 217
  Big Earnings 30
  Enthusiasm 30, 199
  Excitement 30
  Goal-oriented 31
  Grand Ideas 30
  Leadership 30
  Marketing Expertise 199
  Marketing Material 199
  Passion 30
  Payline 200
  Print Newsletters 30
  Top Level 31
  Training 199
DSA 217
Dynamic Compression 71

Breakage 72
Commission Payout 72
Distributor Behavior 72
First-level Distributor 72
Inactive Distributors 72
Level Commissions 72
Motivate 72
Non-qualified Distributors 72
Sales Leaders 72

E

Earnings 7, 42, 50, 51, 52, 56, 57, 61, 62, 64
Earnings Emphasis 217
Earnings Emphasis Commission Plan 185, 188, 192
  Binary 193
  Commission Checks 187
  Commission Percentages 185, 192
  Commission Plan Design 187
  Commissions for Sales 193
  Commission Strategies 193
  Commission Types 186, 192
  Dream-builders 186
  Drifting Between Emphases 189
  Earnings 187
  Group Volume 189
  High-end Emphasis 188, 189, 190
  Earnings Cap Out 190
  Leadership 188
  Level Commissions 192
  Low-end Emphasis 188, 189
  Product Evangelists 188
  Marketing Strategy 189
  Matrix 193
  Mid-range Emphasis 188, 189, 190, 193
  Stable Income 188
  Multiple Commission Types 192
  Not Knowing the Emphasis 189
  Pool Commissions 193
  Product Evangelists 188
  Product Sales 193
  Product Strategy 189
  Rank Advancement 189
  Sales Leaders 186
  Sales Management 193
  Sales Volume 185, 189, 190, 192
  Stable Income 188
  Stairstep 193
  Unigen 193
  Unilevel Commission 193
Earnings Growth 64
Earnings Line 64
Economist 50
Educate 10, 22
Education 3, 8, 10, 11, 12, 13, 15, 18, 206, 207
  Teaching Potential Consumers 10
Employees 6, 38
Employers 38
Enroller 217
Enroller Commission 173
Enroller Tree 112, 118, 176
Enthusiasm 30
Equal-shares Pool 87
Excessive Requirements 57
Excitement 30, 42
Extra $500 a Month 41

F

Fast Start Commissions 125, 129, 170, 180, 209
  Coding Commission 129
  Disadvantage of 130
  First Few Months 129
  Higher Sales Commissions to the Upline 129

New Distributors 129
New Recruit's Sales 129
Recruit's Sales Volume 129
Sponsor 129
Sponsors Incentive 129
Stepped Infinity 129
Unilevel Commission 129
Fiber Supplements. *See also* Products type of
Field Leaders 224
Filling Original Matrix 119
Financial Incentive 58
Financial Independence 42
Financial Planning Service 15
Fine-tune the Commission Plan 210
Finishing Touch Commissions 61, 88
First-generation Leader 157
First Level 217
First-level Commission 163
First Level Distributors 97
  Actual First Level Distributors 97
  First Level with Compression 97
  Qualified Distributors at Specific Rank 97
  Qualified First Level Distributors 97
First Upline Distributor 96
Five Steps to Commission Plan Design
  Commission Payout 50, 51
  Commission Qualifications 48
  Company Mission 48, 49
  Contests and Incentives 48, 58
  Divide Commission Payout 48
  Intellectual Distribution Strategy 49
  Product Price Percentage 50
  Product Stategy 49
  Sales Commissions 51
  Sales Management Commissions 51
Service Strategy 49
Five types of distributors 28
  Consumers 28
  Dream-builders 28
  Product evangelists 28
  Sales leaders 28
  Salespeople 28
Fixed Number of Levels 63
Fixed Percentage 63
Flat Spots 209, 210
Forced Matrix 173. *See also* Limited-width Structure
Forced Structure 218. *See also* Limited-width Structure
Front-end Loading 218
Front-end Loading Schemes 159
Full Commission Payout 73
Future of Commission Plans 205
  Computers 205
  Conference Calls 205
  Intellectual Distribution 206
  Internet 205
  METS Formula 206
  Network Marketing 205
  Operational Issues 205
  Package Shipping 205
  Physical Distribution 206
  Technology 205
  Videos and Audiotapes 205

G

Garage Qualifying 218
Genealogy 218
Generation Commission 62, 63, 65, 66, 67, 104, 157, 158
  Commission Payout 66
  Commission Qualifications 66
  Group Volume 66

Payline 66
Generation Overrides 157
Great Differentiator 16
Group Qualification 56, 57
Group Rank 96
Group Volume 7, 57, 62, 65, 66, 96, 104, 114, 156, 218
  Breakaway Rank 96
  First Upline Distributor 96
  Group Rank 96
  Sponsor 96
Growth 35
GV. *See also* Group Volume

H

Herbal Supplements. *See also* Products type of
Honesty 17
Hoover Vacuum Company 206
Hostess Gifts 155
Hubs of Activity 66, 158
  Challenging Requirements 66
  Compression 66
Hybrid-unilevel Commission 154, 158, 168
  Breakaway 170
  Breakaway Rank 170
  Commission Payout 170
  Commission Percentages 170
  Commission Types 168
  Consumer 168
  Differential Commissions 170
  Dream-builders 168, 169
  Dynamic Compression 169
  Earnings 169
  Fast Start Commissions 170
  Generation Commission 170
  Group Volume 169, 170
  Incentives 168

Infinity 169, 170
  Level Commissions 168, 169
  Low-volume Breakaways 168
  Mini-barrier Plan 170
  Morinda 168
  New Vision International 168
  Open-enrollment 168
  Organization Volume 170
  Payline 171
  Personal Volume 169, 170
  Pool Commissions 169
  Qualification Rules 169, 170
  Qualifying Volume 170
  Rank Advancement 170
  Rebate 170
  Sales Leaders 168, 169
  Salespeople 168
  Salesperson 169
  Sales Volume 170
  Single-level Commissions 170
  Sponsor 170
  Strengths 171
  Tend to Have More Ranks 169
  Top Rank 169
  Unilevels with Fast Starts 168
  Unilevels with Pools 168
  Unilevel with Infinities 168
  Weaknesses 171
Hyper-growth 224

I

Inactive Distributors 70
Incentive Programs 130
  Buy One Get One Free 131
  Contests and Incentives 131
  Free Shipping 131
  Motivate 130
  New Product Promos 131
  Party Plans Companies 131

Index

Product Credit 131
Incentive to Work 50
Income Stability 199
Increased Payout 113
Independent Representatives 4, 5
Infinity 79, 156, 209
Infinity Commission 218
InfoTrax Account Management 229
InfoTrax Systems 229
  DataTrax BackOffice 230
  Distributor Growth 229
  Distributor Retention 229
  Efficient Business Operations 229
  Increased Revenue Per Employee Ratios 229
  Industry Experience 229
  Integrated Communication Tools 231
  Managing Growth of Your Company 229
  Measurable Returns 229
  NetTrax VirtualOffice 230
  Technology Investment 229
  Voice Messaging 231
  WebMeeting 231
Insurance 15
Intellectual Distribution 10, 11, 12, 206, 207
  Sales Commissions 207
Intellectual Distribution Strategy 48, 49
International Commissions 138
  Computer Costs 140
  Ethnic Groups 138
  First-generation Immigrants 138
  Home Country 138
  International Business Policy 140
  International Equivalent of FDA 138
  International Equivalent of IRS 138
  International Sponsorship 140
  Legal Environment 140
  Mass Media Advertising 138
  Network Marketing popularity of 138
  Second-generation Immigrants 138
  Separate Downlines/Separate Commission Plans 139
  Share Product with Relatives 138
  Single Downline/Regionalized Plan 139
  Group Sales Requirements 139
  Personal Sales Requirements 139
  Single Worldwide Downline Unified Commission Plan 138
  Seamless Commission Plan 138
  Unified Commission Plans 139
  Worldwide Commissions 140
International Operations 135
Internet 13, 18, 21, 180, 205, 208, 224, 263
  Company Mission 206
  Competitive Advantage 207
  Downloadable Documents 207
  Educating 180
  Electronic Newsletters 180
  e-mail 180
  Intellectual Distribution 206, 207
  METS Formula 206
  Motivating 180
  Online Learning Libraries 207
  Personal Web Pages 180
  Physical Distribution 206
  Product Demonstration 206
  Supporting 180
  Training 180
  Web Conferencing 207, 208
  WebMeeting 180

Interpersonal Connections 37

J

Job Security 38

L

Lack of Control 38
Laffer Curve 50
Leader Commissions 65. *See also* Generation Commission
Leader Rank. *See also* Group Rank
Leadership 17, 30
Leg 219
Level Commissions 61, 62, 63, 67, 89, 112, 116, 181
   Commission Payout 67
   Commission Plan Rules 69
   Compression 68, 70
   Dynamic Compression 71
   Generation Commission 62, 66
   Group Volume
      Barriers-to-signup 197
      Stairstep 197
      Unigen 197
   Matching Commission 62
   Matrix 116
   Personal Volume
      Hybrid-unilevel Commission 197
      Matrix 197
      Unilevel Commission 197
      Sales Leaders 197
   Sales Volume 67
   Sense of Urgency 67
   Spread Out Earnings 197
   Stable Earnings 197
   Stacking 67, 68
   Unilevel Commission 62, 65
   Levels Paid On 197

Level Volume 96
   Compression 96
   Sales Volume 96
Limited Structure 111
Limited-width Structure 112, 114, 116, 172
   Binary 116, 117
   Matrix 116
   Salespeople 117
   Sponsor 116
   Welfare Mentality 117
Long-distance Sponsoring 118
Long-term Financial Stability 62
Low-volume Breakaways 168

M

Mad Money 40
Magic of the Right Commission Plan 210
Management 3, 47
Marketing Strategy 32, 52, 211
Marketing word of mouth 29
Mark Rawlins Bio 224
Mass Media Advertising 5
Matching Commission 62, 125
   Commission Payout 125
   Enroller Tree 125
   Group Volume 125
   Level Commissions 125
   Matches a Percentage 125
   Motivate 125
   Payline 125
   Percentage of Earnings 125
   Personal Sales Volume 125
   Recruit 125
   Sponsor 125
   Sponsor Tree 125
Matrix 54, 112, 116, 154, 172, 219
   3x9 Structure 173

Index

5x7 Structure 173
Commission Payout 173
Commission Percentages 172
Crossing the Desert 174
Distributor Behavior 174
Earnings 174
Enroller Commission 173
Enroller Tree 172
First-level Distributor 173
Forced Matrix 173
Low Commission Checks 173
Level Commissions 172
Limited-width Structure 172
Multi-center Matrix Plan 172
Personal Volume 172
Qualification Rules 172
Recruit 173
Stacking 173, 174
Strengths 174
Unilevel Commission 172, 173
Weaknesses 174
Media forms of 18
  Audio 18
  CD 18
  Conference Calls 18
  Distributor Kit 18
  International Meetings 18
  Local 18
  Magazine 18
  National 18
  Newsletter 18
  Regional 18
  Video 18
  Web Broadcasting 18
  Web Site 18
Meeting 40
Meetings 29, 30
Methods of Distribution 3
METS Formula 10, 11, 12, 15, 18, 206
  Educate 10

Motivate 10
Support 10
Train 10
Middle-of-the-road Commissions 166
Million-dollar Mansions 42
Mini-barrier Plan 147, 156, 170
  Commission Check 147
  Distributor Price 147
  Preferred Consumer 147
  Preferred Consumer Price 147
  Qualifications 147
  Recruit 147
  Retail Price 147
  Retail Profit 147
Minimum Amount of Structure 112
Minimum Number of Distributors 112
Miscellaneous Commissions 125
  Automobile 125
  Automobile Shared Pool Commissions 126
  Fast Start Commissions 125, 129
  Incentive Programs 130
  Matching Commission 125
Mission 16
MLM 4, 219
Monthly Autoship Volume 97
  Automatically Shipped 97
Monthly Qualification Rules 104
  Commission Percentages 105
  Consumable Product 105
  Dream-builders 105
  Ease of Breaking Away 105
  Generation Commission 104
  Group Volume 104
  Group Volume Requirement 105
  Percent of Potential Consumers 105
  Personal Volume 104

Product Consumption 105
Rank Advancement 104
Sales Leaders 104, 105
Sales Management Commissions 104
Structure Requirements 104
Most Common Plans 151
  Binary 175
  Hybrid-unilevel Commission 168
  Matrix 172
  Sales Commissions First 152
  Stairstep 156
  Unigen 160
  Unilevel Commission 164
Motivate 10, 22, 38, 130
Motivation 3, 8, 10, 12, 13, 15, 17, 18, 39, 206, 207
Motivational CDs 16
Motivational Seminars 16, 37, 39
Motivational Tapes. *See also* Motivational CDs
Multi-center Downline Trees 111, 119, 175
  Binary 119
  Business Center 119
  Business Center Sales Volume 119
  Company-endorsed Stacking 119
  Earnings 119
  Filling Original Matrix 119
  Multiple Commission Checks 119
  New Downline from Center 119
  Scam 120
  Several Positions in Tree 119
Multi-center Matrix Plan 172
Multi-level Commissions
  Differential Commissions 61
  Level Commissions 61, 62
Multi-level Commissions First 153
  Binary 154
  Hybrid-unilevel Commission 154
  Large Downline 153
  Level Commissions 153
  Matrix 154
  Sales Commissions 153
  Sales Leaders 153
  Sales Management Commissions 153
  Unilevel Commission 154
Multi-level Marketing 4
Multilevel Marketing 219
Multiple Countries 136

N

Needs
  Community 37, 58
  Income 37, 38, 58
  Self-improvement 37, 38, 58
Network Marketing 3, 4, 6, 8, 9, 11, 13, 14, 15, 16, 18, 20, 29, 38, 205, 207, 211, 219, 263
Network Marketing Company 4, 6, 27, 36, 37, 38, 39, 52
Non-blocking Commissions 63, 67
Non-qualified Distributors 70
Number of Downline Legs of a Certain Rank 97
  First Level Distributors 97
NuSkin 160, 163

O

Online Learning Libraries 207
Only One Distributor Per Household 106
  Separate Distributorships 107
Open-enrollment 27, 33, 34, 49
  Consumers 142
  Consumer Service 142
  Distributor Wholesale Price 142

Internet Ordering 142
Retail Price 142
Sales Commission 142
Open-enrollment Advantages of 143
Open-enrollment Disadvantages of 143
Open-enrollment Strategy 135, 147, 157
  Consumers 141
  Fairly Compensate the Sales Leaders 142
  Fairly Compensate the Salesperson 142
  Product Evangelist 142
  Recruit 142
  Retail Commission 141
  Salesperson 142
  Sponsor 142
  Strong Sales Commission Strategy 143
  Targeted Campaigns 144
Open Enrollment vs. Barriers-to-Signup 141, 196
  Barriers-to-signup Strategy 141
  Commission Plan 141
  Distributor Wholesale 141
  Open-enrollment Strategy 141
Operational Issues 135, 205
  Barriers-to-signup Strategy 135
  International Commissions 138
  International Operations 135
  Open-enrollment Strategy 135
  Open Enrollment vs. Barriers-to-Signup 141
  Pricing 135
  Pricing Methodologies 135
  Recruit 135
  Reduced Commission Value Products 137
  Optimum Tax Rate 51

Organization Structure 208
Organization Volume 79, 96, 170
Overlapping Infinity 76, 210
Overlapping Infinity Commissions 210

P

Package Shipping 20, 205
Paid Rank 71, 220
Party Order Gifts 155
Party Plan Business 145, 154
  Avon 154
  Barriers-to-signup Strategy 154
  Dream-builders 155
  Incentives and Promotions 155
  Less Commissions to Pay Sales Managers 154
  More Commissions to Pay Salespeople 154
  Multi-level Commissions 154
  Party Plan Rules 155
  Hostess Gifts 155
  Party Order Gifts 155
  Qualifying Volume 155
  Salespeople 154
  Stairstep 154
  Unigen 154
Party Plan Company 4, 6
Party Plan Rules 155
Passion 30
Paying Multi-level Commissions First 151
Paying Salesperson First 151
Payline 56, 64, 66, 158
Peer-to-peer Marketing 135
Percentage of Earnings 125
Perfect Structure 115
Personal Development 16
  Conventions 16

Motivational Seminars 16
Personal Growth 16, 38
  Conventions 16
  Motivational Seminars 16
Personal Sales Volume 96
  Product Line 96
  Sales Leaders 96
Personal Sponsored/Sales Volume 97
Personal Volume 7, 65, 66, 104
Physical Distribution 10, 11, 12, 206, 207
Pin Rank 71, 220
Point Value 219
Pool Commissions 61, 72, 85, 89, 156, 181
  Added Incentive 86
  Car Programs 87
  Commission Payout 86
  Commission Percentages 86
  Earnings 87
  Equal-shares Pool 87
  Finishing Touch Commissions 88
  Motivate 87
  Proportional-shares Pool 87
  Qualification Rules 86
  Rank Advancement 86
  Sales Commission 86
  Sales Management Commissions 86
  Targeting Specific Behavior 85
Price Points 9
Pricing 135
  Commission Plan 135
  Commission Qualifications 136
  Commission Value 136
  Distributor Price 135
  Easy-to-understand Products 135
  Multiple Countries 136
  Peer-to-peer Marketing 135
  Product Line 135
  Published Price List 135
  Qualifying Points 136
  Sponsor 136
  Training 135
  Commission Percentages 135
Pricing Methodologies 135
Private Jets 42
Product 7, 8, 29
  Appropriateness of 9
  Beauty Products 13
  Consumable Product 9
  Diet Products 13
  Education/Training 9
  Health Products 13
  Motivation/Support 9
  Price points 9
  Product Differentiation 14
  Product Does Matter 8
Product Buyback 106
  Restocking Fee 106
Product Delivery 20
Product Demonstration 206
Product Differentiation 14
Product Distribution 3
Product Evangelists 28, 29, 31, 32, 33, 34, 55, 56, 195, 220
  Commission Types 195
  Compensation Strategies 195
  Contests 195
  Differential Commissions 195
  Level Commissions 195
  Multi-month Contest 195
  Non-cash Incentives 195
  Pool Commissions 195
Product Line 9, 19, 51, 96, 135, 211
  Expansion of 9
Product Price Percentage 50
Product Pricing 49
Product Rebate 33, 34

Index

Product Stategy 48, 49
Products type of
  Aloe Vera 14
  Anti-oxidants 14
  Beauty Products 13
  Computer Sales 15
  Diet Products 13
  Fiber Supplements 14
  Financial Planning Service 15
  Health Products 13
  Herbal Supplements 14
  Home Computer 14
  Insurance 15
  Protein Drinks 14
Promote Growth 19
Promote Recruiting 36
Promote Sales 36
Promote Stability 19
Proportional-shares Pool 87
Prorated Pool Commission 200
Protein Drinks 14
PV. *See also* Personal Volume

Q

QP. *See also* Qualifying Points
Qualification Rules 56, 57, 151, 152, 220
  Downline Rank Achievements 96
  Group Volume 96
  Level Volume 96
  Monthly Autoship Volume 97
  Number of Downline Legs of a Certain Rank 97
  Organization Volume 96
  Personal Sales Volume 96
  Personal Sponsored/Sales Volume 97
  Rank Advancement 95
  Receive Commissions 95
  Trained and Certified 97
Qualified 219
Qualified Distributors 112
Qualified Sales Leaders 112, 199
Qualifying Points 136, 219
Qualifying Volume 155
QV. *See also* Qualifying Volume

R

Rank 34, 35, 65, 220
Rank Advancement 55, 67, 94, 104
Rank Advancement Rules 95, 151, 152
  1 Month 100
  Accumulative 100
  Building Downline Organizations 95
  Earnings 95
  Increasing Downline Sales Volume 95
  Multi-month 100
  Top Rank 95
Rebate 170. *See also* Product Rebate
Recruit 7, 28, 29, 31, 32, 35, 36, 114
Reduced Commission Value Products 137
  Commission Percentages 137
  Commission Value 137
  Margin 137
  Price List 137
  Product Line 137
Referral Marketing 167
Remote Sponsoring 155, 220
Required Structure 111
Required Training 144
Required-width Structure 112
  Anti-stacking 114
  Group Volume 114
  Perfect Structure 115

Recruit 114
Sales Leaders 115
Top Rank 115
Retail 35
Retail Commissions 210
Retail Consumer Programs 16
Retail Markup 145
Retail Price 142
Retail Profit 34, 53, 167, 193
Retail Sales Requirements 145
Retention 32, 40
Reversion 101, 220
  Commission Payout 101
  Compression 101
  How Long to Hold a Rank 101
  Paid at a Lower Rank 101
  Permanent Rank 101
  Reduced in Rank 101
  Too Lax 101
  Too Severe 101
  Too Strict 101
Rewarding Distributor Activities 208
Rewarding Dream-builders 208
Rewarding Sales Leaders 208
Rollup 74
  Breakage 74
  Commission Percentages 75
  Compression 74
  Full Commission Payout 75
  Non-qualified Distributors 74
  Qualification Rules 75
  Sales Volume 75
  Sponsor 75
  Stacking 75
  Upline Qualified Distributor 74

S

Sales 3
Sales Commission 142
Sales Commissions 32, 33, 34, 36, 51, 55, 207
  Consumer 194
  Product Evangelists 194
  Salesperson 194
Sales Commissions First 152
  Adding MLM Commissions After Fact 152
  Administrative Burdens 152
  Beginning of Modern Network Marketing 152
  Breakaway 152, 153
  Breakaway Distributor 152
  Commission Calculation 152
  Direct Distributors 152
  Direct Shipping from Home Office 152
  Distribution 152
  Group Volume 152
  Paying Commissions 152
  Qualification Rules 152
  Rank Advancement Rules 152
  Sales Commissions 152, 153
  Sales Management Commissions 152, 153
  Stairstep 154
  Technological Innovations 152
  Technological Limitations 152
  Time to Sell 152
  Time to Support 152
  Time to Train 152
  Unigen 154
  Warehoused Product 152

Index

Sales Force 52
Sales Kit 27
Sales Leader Retention 30
Sales Leaders 19, 28, 29, 31, 34, 43, 52, 56, 61, 66, 105, 112, 172, 221
  Conference Calls 199
  Earnings 199
  Income Stability 199
  Meetings 199
  Mid-range Emphasis 199
  Motivate 199
  Pool Commissions 199
  Qualified Sales Leaders 199
  Targeted Commissions 199
  Training 199
Sales Management 52
Sales Management Commissions 32, 33, 34, 51, 55, 56, 63, 67, 104, 152, 197
  Binary 197
  Commission Payout 200
  Mid-range Emphasis 200
  Commission Percentages 197
  Compression 198
  Dream-builders 199
  Enthusiasm 199
  Marketing Expertise 199
  Marketing Material 199
  Payline 200
  Training 199
  Earnings 198
  Group Volume 197, 198
  Hubs of Activity 198
  Incentive Programs 198
  Infinity 200
  Level Commissions 197
  Sales Leaders 197
  Spread Out Earnings 197
  Stable Earnings 197
  Levels Paid On 197
  Miscellaneous Commissions 199
  Pool Commissions 197, 198
  Prorated Pool Commission 200
  Qualification Rules 198
  Sales Leaders 197, 199
    Conference Calls 199
    Meetings 199
    Mid-range Emphasis 199
    Motivate 199
    Pool Commissions 199
    Qualified Sales Leaders 199
    Targeted Commissions 199
    Training 199
  Single-level Group Volume 199
  Targeting Specific Behavior 198
  Top Rank 198
Sales Meetings 39
Salespeople 4, 6, 19, 28, 29, 32, 33, 35, 40, 66
  Income Stability 199
Salesperson 31, 36, 52, 55, 61, 195
  Barriers-to-signup 196
  Commission Percentages 197
  Earnings 196
  Open Enrollment vs. Barriers-to-Signup 196
  Qualification Rules 197
  Rank Advancement 197
  Recruit 196
  Retail Profit 196
  Sales Commission 196
  Support Product Evangelists 196
Salesperson - Hostess - Attendees 145
Sales Volume 56, 64, 96, 112, 209
Scam 8, 120
Second Income 40
Self-Fulfilling Prophecy 43
Sell Product 36

283

Sense of Belonging 37
  Less Emphasis on Family 37
  Population is Mobile 37
  Religious Structures 37
  Tribal People 37
  Workplace is Volatile 37
Sense of Community 37
Sense of Purpose 37
Services 7, 8, 16
Service Strategy 48, 49
Services type of
  Business-building 16
  Personal Development 16
  Personal Growth 16
Several Positions in Tree 119
Simple is Always Better 165
Single Downline/Regionalized Plan
  Sales Volume Requirements 139
Single-level Commissions 61, 82, 89, 163, 181
  Benefits of 84
  Breakaway 85
  Commission Payout 83
  Commission Percentages 83, 84
  Commission Types 84
  Differential Commissions 83
  Disadvantages of 84
  Group Volume 83
  Level Commissions 84
  Qualification Rules 83
  Rank 83
  Sales Leaders 83
  Salesperson 83
  Sales Volume 85
  Variable Earnings 84
Social Needs 16
Socio-economic Background 19
Sponsor 27, 33, 52, 98, 116, 221
Sponsoring Regulation 221
Sponsors and Enrollers 111, 118

Commission Payout 119
Commission Types 118
Complexity of Commission Plan 118
Enroller Tree 118
Incentive to Sponsor 118
Long-distance Sponsoring 118
Sponsor Tree 118
Two Downline Trees 118
Sponsor Tree 118
Spread-the-wealth Tool 62
Stability of a Company 39, 40
Stable Earnings 62, 67, 81, 208
Stacking 67, 68, 75, 113, 221
  Enforcement 69
Stairstep 76, 78, 154, 156
  Automobile Shared Pool Commissions 157
  Breakaway 157
  Commission Types 156, 159
  Differential Commissions 156
  Level Commissions 156
  Compression 158
  Consumers 79
  Differential Commissions 157, 160
  Dream-builders 156
  First-generation Leader 157
  Forever Living 156
  Front-end Loading Schemes 159
  Generation Commission 157, 158
  Generation Overrides 157
  Group Volume 78, 156, 158, 159
  Hubs of Activity 158
  Hybrid-unilevel Commission 158
  Infinity 156
  Level Commissions 158
  Meadow Fresh 156
  Open-enrollment Strategy 157
  Payline 158
  Personal Volume 78

Pool Commissions 156, 157
Product Evangelists 79, 156, 157
Qualification Rules 159
Sales Leaders 156, 157
Sales Management Commissions 156, 158, 159
Salespeople 78, 159
Salesperson 156
Sponsor 157
Technology 156
Unilevel Commission 158
Unqualified Leaders 158
Standard Commissions Plans 151, 154
Stepped Infinity 79
  Blocking Commissions 79
  Commission Percentages 79
  Dream-builders 79
  Organization Volume 79
Stretch Limousines 42
Structure 221
Structured Commission Plans
  Binary 54
  Limit First-level Distributors 54
  Matrix 54
  Multiple Positions in Tree 54
  Structured Downline 54
Structure Requirement 113
Structure Requirements types of 114
  Limited-width Structure 114
  Required-width Structure 114
Support 8, 10, 11, 12, 13, 15, 18, 22, 206
SV. *See also* Sales Volume

T

Targeted Commissions 55
  Differential Commissions 193
  Pool Commissions 193

Single-level Commissions 193
Targeted to Sales People 193
Targeting Specific Behavior 85, 198
Tax Rate 50
Tax Revenue 51
Technology 20, 22, 61, 156, 205
Telecommunications Revolution 21
Telemarketing 5
Test Commission Plans 209
Top Rank 95, 98, 112, 115
Town Meetings 37
Traditional Network Marketing Business 154, 155
  Commission Types 155
  Enroller Tree 155
  Internet 155
  Mini-barrier Plan 156
  Remote Sponsoring 155
Traditional Sales 3, 5
Train 10, 22
Train Corporate Staff 210
Trained and Certified 97
Training 3, 8, 11, 12, 13, 15, 18, 39, 206, 207
Tree 221
Two Downline Trees 118
Two First Levels 175
Two Types of Rules 93
  Negative Rules 93
  Positive Rules 93

U

Unified Commission Plans 139
Unigen 154, 160
  Breakaway 164
  Cernitin 162
  Commission Payout 160, 161
  Commission Types 160, 164
  Level Commissions 160

Understanding Multi-Level Commissions

Single-level Commissions 160
Compromise Plan 164
Consumers 163
Dream-builders 161, 163
First-level Commission 163
Group Volume 160, 161, 163
Infinity 160
Level Commissions 160, 161, 163
NuSkin 160, 163
Pay Worldwide Commissions 164
Personal Volume 160
Pool Commissions 160
Preferred Consumers 163
Product Evangelists 161
Simple Level Commission 161
Professional Distributors 163
Register Every Consumer 164
Retail Consumers 163
Retail Sales 163
Sales Leaders 161, 163
Sales Management Commissions 160, 161
Salespeople 160, 163
Salesperson 161
Solid Commission 161
Single-level Commissions 160, 163
Strengths 163
Two Commission Types 164
Variable Percentage Single-level Commission 161
Weaknesses 164
Unigen advantages of 163
Unilevel Commission 62, 65, 154, 158, 164, 221, 236
Barriers-to-signup 167
Commission Payout 165
Commission Percentages 166
Commission Types 165
Compression 165
Earnings 167
Easy to Understand 167
Group Volume 165
Hybrid-unilevel Commission 167
Level Commissions 165
Middle-of-the-road Commissions 166
One Commission Type 165
Payline 167
Personal Volume 165
Qualification Rules 165
Rank 165
Rank Advancement 166
Referral Marketing 167
Retail Profit 167
Sales Management Commissions 165, 167
Salespeople 165, 167
Simple is Always Better 165
Spreads the Wealth 167
Stacking 167
Strengths 167
Weaknesses 167
Unilevels with Fast Starts 168
Unilevels with Pools 168
Unilevel with Dynamic Compression 249
Unilevel with Infinities 168
Unilevel with No Compression 238
Unilevel with Standard Compression 242
Unstructured Commission Plans 54
Unlimitted First-level Distributors 54
Upline 221
Upline Qualified Distributor 74
Upline Sales Leader 57

V

Value Proposition 30
Variable Percentage Single-level
 Commission 161
Videos and Audiotapes 21, 205

W

Wal-Mart 206
Web-based Training 16
Web Conferencing 207, 208
Wholesale price 28
Wholesale Price 145

Understanding Multi-Level Commissions